Song
of
Songs

Come Away My Beloved

An Interpretation of the Song of Solomon

James T. Harman

Prophecy
Countdown
Publications

Song of Songs – Come Away My Beloved

Copyright © 2016, James T. Harman

Prophecy Countdown Publications, LLC
P.O. Box 941612
Maitland, FL 32794
www.ProphecyCountdown.com

ISBN: 978-0-9636984-8-3

All references from Scripture are from the King James Version unless noted otherwise: ESV – English Standard Version®, copyright ©2001 Crossway
    NAS – New American Standard Bible, copyright ©1960
    NIV – New International Version, copyright ©1973
    NKJV– New King James Version, copyright ©1982
    HCSB– Holman Christian Standard Bible®, registered trademark
        and copyright © 2009, by Holman Bible Publishers
    AMP – Amplified Bible, copyright ©1987 Lockman Foundation
        AMP Old Testament © 1987 the Zondervan Corporation
    CDG – Christian D. Ginsburg paraphrase, published in 1857

Scripture abbreviations as used throughout this book are from the Blue Letter Bible (www.BlueLetterBible.org), and they are summarized on p. 84. Numerical references to selected words in the text of Scripture are from James H. Strong Dictionaries of the Hebrew and Greek words.

Words in bold emphasis are authors and not in original Scripture. Certain words such as Kingdom and Judgment Seat of Christ are capitalized to emphasize their importance, but not in accordance with traditional fashions. Certain numerical values are used for clarity or emphasis in presentation and not in accordance with guidelines recommended by all traditional practices.

NOTE TO READER

The purpose of this writing is not to provide a verse-by-verse commentary of the entire Song of Songs. Many other authors have provided such works. The main objective of this book is to focus on helping the reader discover the wonderful message God has for us in this most beautiful Song for His faithful beloved bride.

Throughout this book, bibliographical references may be provided in the comments on selected texts with the commentator's last name along with page numbers (in parenthesis) for the references cited.

Come Away My Beloved by Jim Harman has been written with grace, precision, and fidelity to the scriptures. While many books purporting to "interpret" the Song of Solomon range from imaginative to bizarre, Jim's work is clear, coherent, and most important: applicable. Jim has revealed the eschatological significance of the Song of Solomon in a delightful way. If you are excited about the Lord's soon return and have wondered whether there is a message for the church in the Old Testament, I highly recommend this book.   Steve Coerper – Raleigh, NC
Anakypto Forum

Thank you for your new book, *Come Away My Beloved*. I love the way you tied the Lord preparing His Bride for His return with the Song of Songs! May it serve as a love call to all of God's saints to prepare their hearts for the coming King! Even so, come Lord Jesus!   Steve Gallagher – Dry Ridge, KY
Author of *The Time of Your Life In Light of Eternity*

In the pages of this short commentary you will discover new insights into comprehending the message of the Song of Songs. You will come to appreciate, as we have, how the author's arduous research and study has enabled him to bring together a fresh approach in the spiritual understanding and truths of this beautiful portion of God's word. Do take the time to savor it!
Lewis Schoettle, Ed. D.
and Charlotte Schoettle – Haysville, NC

Come Away My Beloved is a treat for the Bible student on the Song of Solomon. Fresh, warm, and sensitive, this deeply thought-out volume will spur thinking and give prophetic insights. Whether you subscribe to the three-character theory of the Song or not, you will be greatly enriched by this fine book.
Jimmy Reagan – Leesville, SC

The Song of Songs is the most wonderful love story, ever, ever written. *Come Away My Beloved* is a great tribute to it.
Gerry Almond – Swansea, IL

Jim Harman's new book, *Come Away My Beloved* will be a great benefit for Christian formation classes dealing with the lifelong process of growing in our relationship with God, self and others; and learning ways to live a sometimes countercultural life in a secular world. It is both approachable and yet scholarly. James W. Ross, MD – Providence Forge, VA

Come Away My Beloved is a story that demonstrates a Godly way to have a romance between a man and a woman. A second and even more important aspect of this book is that its prophetic interpretation gives all Christians very easy to understand encouragement to remain faithful to Jesus Christ.
Eric Summers – Ooltewah, TN
First Fruits Ministry

Through the Spirit-guided pen of James Harman, you will experience a new love for and devotion to Christ as you read his inspired interpretation of the Song of Solomon. Fortified with such devotion and love, *Come Away My Beloved* will help insure your participation in the coming marriage to Christ as part of His bride. Charles F. Strong – Harlingen, TX
Bible One Ministry

I really benefitted from Jim Harman's new book, *Come Away My Beloved.* For the first time the Song of Solomon became clear to me, while also revealing many prophetic aspects for believers within this beautiful love story. Any Christian that has an opportunity to read this new book will truly be inspired by the True Lover of our Souls, and be drawn to Him in a sweet, reverent, and intimate way. Judith Stack – Port Orange, FL

Come Away My Beloved is simply beautiful – illustrating the love and fulfillment only God can give and that every soul longs for. It covers the scriptural requirements for one seeking to be part of the Bridehood Saints of Christ – in Spirit and in Truth – from the call to the consummation – what a day that will be!!!
"Eye has not seen nor ear heard the things God has prepared for those who love Him." Joan Olsen – Oklahoma City, OK

Prologue

The Song of Solomon is one of the most perplexing books in the Bible. Next to the book of Revelation, it is among the most difficult books to understand. The Song's difficultly partially stems from the fact that when a person reads the narrative for the very first time the identity of the various speakers are not always given. This is further complicated by the fact that many different Bible translators mistakenly change the entire plot just by making a faulty judgement as to the correct speaker.

The Song is also one of the most debated and misunderstood books in all of Scripture. Countless numbers of interpretations have led to much confusion, forcing many to avoid the book entirely. This commentary will not be a verse-by-verse exegesis, but is intended to provide the readers with a fresh look at this most delightful story of love.

This author struggled with understanding the Song's true meaning because the traditional interpretation revolves around the king's love for a Shulamite maiden and her supposed love for him. This two character storyline is the predominate view taken by most expositors; however, many people are confused as to how this could possibly represent true love when Solomon shared his life with over 1,000 different women. Even from a spiritual perspective, how could Solomon's life represent Christ as a true type? His polygamy could hardly characterize the righteous love our heavenly Bridegroom has for His bride.

After years of reading and studying numerous commentaries, I too was puzzled as to what the Song of Songs' true meaning really is. Then I came across an interpretation that explained the Song as a love story that revolves around the three primary characters: Solomon, the Shulamite maiden, and her shepherd lover (see Appendix 2). This important perspective became the key clue to uncloak its mystery and reveal its actual meaning.

Understanding this true storyline will assist the reader in following the narrative, which at first glance, has little or no logical sequence. The Song becomes a beautiful romance that unfolds with seven major players telling the story of how a young girl fell in love with a young shepherd boy. Their strong love for one another proved to be true love that God had placed in their hearts – they were indeed soulmates devoted to each other. Their great love was able to withstand all of the trials of being separated along with being tempted by the lure of King Solomon's magnificent wealth and power. In the end, the devotion and faithfulness of the Shulamite maiden proves no match for the life Solomon offered her. Her loyalty and commitment to her betrothed demonstrates a great lesson from which all of God's people can learn.

While the Song is a great love story between a man and a woman, one of its purposes is to remind believers that we too are espoused to our heavenly Bridegroom who went away to prepare a place for us. While He is gone, we reside in a world (a foreign land that is not our home) where we are tested and tempted every day to forsake Him.

Another object of this Song is to reveal vital prophetic admonitions for followers of Christ that many may have missed. One of the main purposes of this book is to help bring these important truths to light in order to help the Church prepare for their glorious wedding day when Jesus returns for His bride.

At Christ's return he will be seeking a people willing to forsake the world for their love and devotion to Him. May this short work revive your heart with a fervent love for your Saviour. May this inspirational Song arouse your spirit in order to hear the Spirit's passionate cry to come away with Him:

"Rise up, my love, my fair one, and come away"
(Song of Songs 2:10)

Dedication

This book is dedicated to Dorothy Spaulding, the artist who painted the beautiful painting of the Bride, which adorns the front cover of this book. Dorothy's painting has inspired countless numbers of people into looking for the blessed hope of Christ's return for their beloved Saviour. May her inspirational rendering of the Lord's return stir your heart to join in the impassioned cry with the rest of the bride:

"Make haste, my beloved, and come quickly..."
(Song of Songs 8:14 – AMP)

"...Looking for that blessed hope,
and the glorious appearing
of the great God and
our Saviour Jesus Christ..."
(Titus 2:13)

Contact information for the artist who painted *The Bride*:

Dorothy Spaulding
Watchmen Broadcasting
P.O. Box 36185
Augusta, GA 30914
803-278-3618
www.wbpi.org

Storyline of the Song of Songs

The Seven
Major Players: King Solomon,
the Shulamite maiden,
her shepherd lover,
the court ladies (also known as
the daughters of Jerusalem),
the inhabitants of Jerusalem,
the brothers of the Shulamite,
the companions of the shepherd.

The Song of Solomon, which is also known as the Song of Songs, is divided into eight chapters. When properly understood, it reveals an exquisite story of love and faithfulness. The following storyline was developed over 100 years ago by a prominent Hebrew scholar, well known for his textual and critical study of the Old Testament:

"A beautiful Shulamite maiden, surprised by the king and his train on a royal progress in the north ($6^{11\text{-}12}$), has been brought to the palace at Jerusalem [$3^{6\text{-}11}$ &c.], where the king hopes to win her affections, and to induce her to exchange her rustic home for the honour and enjoyments which a court life could afford. She has, however, already pledged her heart to a young shepherd; and the admiration and blandishments which the king lavishes upon her are powerless to make her forget him. In the end she is permitted to return to her mountain home, where, at the close of the poem, the lovers appear hand in hand (8^5), and express, in warm and glowing words, the superiority of genuine, spontaneous affection over that which may be purchased by wealth or rank ($8^{6\text{-}7}$)."[1]

The convention of verse citation employed by the above author will be used throughout this book. In citations, the letters [a] and [b] denote the first and second halves of the verse cited.

Table of Contents

Foreword

There are two significant attributes to the latest presentation by Jim Harman—the first his deep and devoted love of our Lord that is clearly present on every page. The second is that Jim takes the Song of Solomon, which has always been confusing and misunderstood, and with one simply yet profound revolution, reveals it to be one of the most loving and meaningful messages in the Bible.

For over 25 years I have found Jim's work to display a whole new dimension in biblical understanding. Similar to adding the dimension of depth to a two-dimensional drawing, Jim was able to realize, and adeptly demonstrate, that the Song of Solomon was not written about the king and his would be concubine, but rather is the love story of the bride (the church of faithful believers), the king (the world trying to seduce her), and her true love (our Lord).

By simply, yet eloquently, identifying the three characters this ancient work at last makes sense and does so in a most beautiful and meaningful way.

John Zajac
Scientist and author of
The Delicate Balance

Exposition on the Book of Canticles
By Charles H. Spurgeon

"We will this evening read in the one Book of the Bible which is wholly given up to fellowship; I allude to the Book of Canticles. This Book stands like the tree of life in the midst of the garden, and no man shall ever be able to pluck its fruit, and eat thereof, until first he has been brought by Christ past the sword of the cherubim, and led to rejoice in the love which hath delivered him from death. The Song of Solomon is only to be comprehended by the men whose standing is within the veil. The outer-court worshippers, and even those who only enter the court of the priests, think the Book a very strange one; but they who some very near to Christ can often see in this Song of Solomon the only expression which their love to their Lord desires."

The above excerpt from Sermon No. 2469 delivered on June 14th, 1896 at the Metropolitan Tabernacle, Newington, provided courtesy of the Blue Letter Bible: (www.blbclassic.org)

Introduction

We are about to explore one of the most passionate love stories of all time. With explicit dialogue between a young woman and her lover, we will witness the wonderful joys of love and romance experienced by two young people who cherish one another; dedicated to each other's happiness.

The Song of Solomon was written almost 3,000 years ago and it contains timeless teachings of virtue and faithfulness that exemplify the ideals everyone should aspire to. Even more importantly, this brilliant song of love reflects God's desire for every man and woman; not only in their present lives but also in their relationship with Him.

Readers are encouraged to review Appendix 1 to discover the various techniques of interpretation that have been utilized to help explain the Song's meaning. Ever since the early Church Fathers banned the literal method in 550 AD, both Jewish and Christian expositors have predominately used the allegorical manner of interpretation. In order to appreciate its full message, this short work will approach the Song in an eclectic manner because we believe there are literal, figurative, and prophetic aspects that need to be recognized.

Who wrote, and when the Song was written, are just as controversial as to how it should be interpreted. These matters are beyond the purpose of this book since the answers are less important than its overall theme. Because we believe there are three primary characters: Solomon, the Shulamite maiden, and her shepherd lover, we also doubt that Solomon was the author. It may be possible that the king wrote the song in the waning years of his life as he reflected over his shortcomings and failures. But this explanation is diminished by the fact that the king would hardly announce that his own creation was *the finest and most celebrated Song,* [2] as made in the opening line of the Song, which begins with: *"The song of songs [the most excellent of them all] which is Solomon's."* (Sgs 1:1 – AMP)

The phrase, *"the song of songs"* represents a superlative similar to the Scriptures that state: *'King of kings'* or *'Lord of lords.'* This Song therefore represents the best or the most excellent of all songs ever written.[3]

Many believe the phrase, *"which is Solomon's"* suggests *'belonging to Solomon'* (*cf.* 1Ki 10:26-28) or *'concerning Solomon'* in a more general way (*cf.* 1Ki 5:15); therefore the song was probably written about the king and not written by King Solomon. So this song contains one of the best songs ever written and it pertains to the life of one of the wisest men who ever lived (*cf.* 1Ki 4:29-31). Unfortunately, Solomon's major flaws of disobeying God and his pursuit of worldly pleasure led to his ultimate downfall (*cf.* 1Ki 11:1-8). Instead of Solomon being a type representing Christ or godly principles, his role in the story depicts him as a negative prototype symbolizing worldly wealth, pleasure, and power.

The true heroine of the Song becomes the humble shepherdess who is devoted to her one true love. Most of the Song revolves around her character; making this important book unified by the influence of this woman of virtue and devotion. The author of the concluding Proverb must have recognized her marvelous worth when he wrote:

> *"Who can find a virtuous woman? for her price is far above rubies"* (Pro 31:10).

The young Shulamite maiden was indeed such a woman. Her life is a magnificent portrait of virtue and love, demonstrating devotion and faithfulness to her betrothed; a perfect role model for all people of God to emulate. May her passion ignite a flame in your heart as you read her beautiful love story.

Act 1 – Love Between Two Lovers

Shulamite in royal tent separated from her beloved shepherd.
(Song of Songs 1:2 to 2:7)

Scene 1 (1$^{2-8}$)
(Shulamite maiden and court ladies in Solomon's royal tent.)
The story opens with the beautiful maiden before the court ladies after she had been taken to the king's tent in the country. She had recently been engaged to a shepherd boy to whom she has pledged her heart. One day she went into the garden (6$^{11-12}$) looking for fruits and herbs when she unwittingly ran into the presence of the king. Captivated by her beauty, King Solomon brought her to his summer retreat, where the story begins.

Shulamite

"2) Let him kiss me with the kisses of his mouth: for thy love is better than wine. 3) Because of the savour of thy good ointments thy name is as ointment poured forth, therefore do the virgins love thee" (Sgs 1:2-3).

The young maiden begins her soliloquy[1] about her innermost feelings for her beloved shepherd because she longs to be with him instead of being in King Solomon's residence. She wishes her fiancé were present so she could enjoy his sweet kisses and delight in his pleasant fragrance. All of the other young women adore the companion to which she is espoused.

These verses also picture the first love the believer has for the Lord. All the faithful love Him and desire His presence more than anything the world can offer. The Shulamite's cry for her lover speaks to our longing for intimacy with Jesus, our Savior.

"Oh draw me after thee! Oh let us flee together!
The king has brought me into his apartments, But we exult and
rejoice in thee, We praise thy love more than wine,
The upright love thee" (Sgs 1:4 – CDG).

She continues her discourse with the desire to run away with her shepherd lover, acknowledging that it was the king who had taken her away from her home. While the intent of the king is to attempt to win her love though seductive flatteries, she is telling her audience that her love is far greater than wine; a facet all virtuous maidens acknowledge.

Her desire to return to her true love is pictured by the call of all upright virgins represented by the bride of Christ as seen in the book of Revelation: *"And the Spirit and the bride say, Come. And let him that heareth say, Come"* (Rev 22:17). The Shulamite's yearning to leave the king's chambers (a type of the world) corresponds to our plea to leave this world (which is not our true home) so we can be with the One we love.

"5) I am dark, but lovely, O daughters of Jerusalem, Like the
tents of Kedar, Like the curtains of Solomon. 6) Do not look
upon me, because I am dark, Because the sun has tanned me.
My mother's sons were angry with me; They made me the
keeper of the vineyards, But my own vineyard I have not kept."
(Sgs 1:5-6 – NKJV)

Realizing the court ladies are giving her scornful stares (because of her dark complexion), she explains to them that her step-brothers made her work in the family's vineyard, and the hot sun has given her a dark tan. These last two verses are really a pause in her discourse to the court ladies, telling them about how she had been taken into the king's tent, and her desire to return to her home to be with her true love. She now resumes her soliloquy by contemplating her shepherd lover and thinking about where she can find him in order to be reunited.

*"Tell me, O thou **whom my soul loveth**, Where thou feedest thy
flock, Where thou causest it to lie down at noon,
Lest I should be roaming Among the flocks of thy companions. "*
(Sgs 1:7 – CDG)

The young maiden clearly is seeking the whereabouts of her
young shepherd who is her soulmate. Only a shepherd would
be one pasturing a flock of sheep to escape the heat of the noon
day sun by taking shelter (*cf.* Gen 29:7, Psa 23). This verse,
along with the following reply by the court ladies, is rather
convincing proof that the Shulamite is looking for a shepherd
and not the king, who was not likely to be seen tending sheep.

Court Ladies
*"8) If thou know not, O thou **fairest among women**, go thy way
forth by the footsteps of the flock,
and feed thy kids beside the shepherds' tents"* (Sgs 1:8).

*"8) If you do not know [where your lover is], O you **fairest
among women**, run along, follow the tracks of the flock, and
[amuse yourself by] pasturing your kids beside the shepherds'
tents"* (Sgs 1:8 – AMP).

The court ladies are the only ones to address the young maiden
as the *"fairest among women"* (*cf.* Sgs 6^1). After hearing her
request to find her beloved shepherd, they almost sarcastically
tell her to go ahead and give up the life of comfort and ease the
king is about to offer her, and return to the life of a shepherdess.

Scene 2 (1^9- 2^7)
(Solomon enters with the Shulamite maiden and court ladies.)
Having heard the court ladies' reply to the young maiden,
King Solomon briefly enters the chamber in his royal tent.
This is his initial attempt to try to lure her away from her
rustic life, which he begins by flatteries and enticing offers.

Solomon

"9) To me, my darling, you are like My mare among the chariots of Pharaoh. 10) Your cheeks are lovely with ornaments, Your neck with strings of beads. 11) We will make for you ornaments of gold With beads of silver."
(Sgs 1:9-11 – NAS)

Having heard the beautiful young maiden describe how she had acquired such a dark tan (in reply to the scornful glances (1^{5-6}) by the court ladies), Solomon turned their disdain around into a flattering complement. He viewed her dark tan as something to be admired. Solomon saw her dark complexion as a thing of great beauty. The king owned over 12,000 horses (2Ch 9:25), many that he obtained from Egypt, which were considered to be the finest horses one could own. Only the best horses would be selected for Pharaoh's chariots, so the king is comparing her to the best of the best. As pointed out by Ginsburg, the king was comparing her to his prized "steed, whose dark color renders it more beautiful than the other horses. Such a comparison must have been very striking and flattering…this animal was so much celebrated for its preeminent beauty."[2]

The king continues his flatteries by commenting on her beautiful cheeks and her charming neck. The young maiden had been endowed with natural beauty and the king was captivated by her gorgeous appearance. He admires her attractive jewelry and how it complements her innate loveliness. He now offers to bestow on this humble country girl the finest and costliest ornaments his great kingdom can provide. He is offering her jewelry fashioned in pure gold and silver. He is promising to lavish her with the finest things in his initial effort to lure her away from her rustic life in the country. His opening attempt is very brief, but is meant to dazzle her with his adulations of her notable beauty and his enticing promises to give her possessions beyond anything she could ever hope to receive from her humble shepherd boy.

The young maiden's first trial by the king is symbolic of the believer's temptation by the world to lure us away from our devotion to the good Shepherd (*cf.* Jhn 10:11,14, Heb 13:20, 1Pe 2:25).[3] The Shulamite is espoused to her beloved shepherd, but Solomon came into her chamber with the intent of wooing her away from him. In a similar manner, the things of this world (1Jo 2:15-16) attempt to distract us from the Lord, away from the life He desires for us.

Shulamite
"12) While the king sits at his table [she said], my spikenard [my absent lover] sends forth [his] fragrance [over me].
13) My beloved [shepherd] is to me like a [scent] bag of myrrh that lies in my bosom. 14) My beloved [shepherd] is to me a cluster of henna flowers in the vineyards of En-gedi [famed for its fragrant shrubs]" (Sgs 1:12-14 – AMP).

Fortunately, once the king has finished enticing her, the young maiden immediately turns her attention and her thoughts to her beloved shepherd. The king exits her tent and reclines at his own table, leaving the Shulamite alone with the court ladies. She turns her feelings back toward her absent lover, and continues her discourse, calling him *"my spikenard"* (#5373 *nard*), which is a plant that gives off a distinctive and pleasing aroma. Remember that when Jesus was in Bethany, a woman had a very precious ointment of *spikenard,* with which she anointed him (Mar 14:3). By using this name for her lover, the young maiden is telling us that her beloved is very cherished and precious to her.

She then continues describing him using metaphors of other sweet smelling items: *a bag of myrrh* and *henna flowers.* A bag of *myrrh* was frequently worn on a necklace, which would dangle between a woman's breasts, close to her heart. The wonderful fragrance of this costly perfume reminds her of her beloved when he is not around. Of course *myrrh* was one of the treasured gifts the wise men gave when they visited Jesus in the manger, and it was also used in His burial. The Shulamite kept the *myrrh* close to her heart as a reminder of how precious her espoused is to her. This a beautiful picture to remind us how dear the Lord is to the believer. *Myrrh* reminds us of His marvelous birth and His glorious resurrection. In His absence, we have the treasured gift of the Word, which we hide in our hearts (*cf.* Psa 119:9-16) and can experience intimate fellowship with Him every day until we are reunited with Him.

She also compares her beloved to a *cluster of henna flowers* (*cf.* Sgs 4^{13}, 7^{13}). These flowers were the most beautiful and sweet smelling plants, which could be found in the gardens of *En-gedi,* an oasis west of the Dead Sea. These delightful flowers came from a shrub that protected the vineyards from erosion and unwanted animals. *En-gedi* sprang-up from a fresh spring near the barren wilderness, allowing these fragrant flowers to flourish. Her adored shepherd represents a sanctuary of shelter and protection she longs to embrace, and these famed flowers symbolize the security and care he provides.

The Shulamite is telling us how much her beloved means to her and how very much she loves and cherishes him. This virtuous maiden is teaching us a very valuable lesson. Whenever we are tempted by the things of this world, we should immediately turn our attention to the good Shepherd. Jesus is our refuge. His words are sweeter than honey (Psa 119:103), and He provides us a very present help we can turn to in our time of need (Heb 4:16). He represents a safe haven we can turn to anytime we are tempted, and His love for us is our most cherished possession.

[The Shepherd]***
"Behold, you are beautiful, my love!
Behold, you are beautiful!
You have doves' eyes" (Sgs 1:15 – AMP).
***[Shulamite repeats words her beloved shepherd once spoke.]

After the king left her tent and she reflected on her beloved shepherd, she now remembers him telling her how beautiful she is to him: that her eyes remind him of a dove. The dove is a symbol of purity, innocence, and fidelity; qualities the humble maiden exudes and which her beloved highly esteemed.

Shulamite
"16) Behold thou art comely, my beloved. Yea thou art lovely; verdant is our couch, 17) Our bower is our cedar arches, Our retreat of cypress roof. 1) I am a mere flower of the plain, A lily of the valley" (Sgs 1:16-17, 2:1 – CDG).

The maiden continues her dialogue before the court ladies by saying that he is the handsome one. She reflects on how appealing he is, which reminds her of the place where they would meet. Most of the translations use the word "house" (#1004 *bayith*), however, in context, Ginsberg's paraphrase as a *"bower"* gives us a clearer picture of what this verse is telling us. A bower is a shady, leafy shelter that is frequently nestled among plants and trees in a garden or other wooded areas. Here, this bower represents a pleasant secluded place where the couple would meet. It was their coveted rendezvous, an attractive retreat with beautiful foliage where they could meet to be alone; a place where they shared many times of intimate devotion to one another.

She then compares herself to a mere flower in the valley. She sees herself as a common ordinary wildflower growing in the field. Her humble character is one of the most endearing traits that she possesses, one that he greatly admires, and one the good Shepherd highly prizes as well (*cf.* Isa 66:2, Mat 5:5).

[The Shepherd]***
"Like a lily among the thorns, So is my darling among the maidens" (Sgs 2:2 – NAS).
***[Shulamite repeats words her beloved shepherd once spoke.]

Her beloved shepherd doesn't see her as just another ordinary wildflower, but he sees his humble young maiden as a beautiful lily growing among thorns. He highly values her meek spirit and is charmed by her exquisite beauty. He sees her as the most beautiful of all the young maidens. To him, she is a beautiful lily far exceeding all the others.

In the same way, our beloved Shepherd also sees the pure and trusting lily to be of far more beauty and worth than all of Solomon's glory:

> *"28)...Consider the lilies of the field, how they grow: they neither toil nor spin; 29) and yet I say to you that even Solomon in all his glory was not arrayed like one of these."*
> (Mat 6:28-29 – NKJV)

The beautiful lilies graced the countryside with a divine magnificence that even the most expensive robes of the king could not compare. In Christ's Sermon on the Mount, He used the humble lilies[4] to teach us how the pure and humble totally trust and rely upon Him as the source of all their needs. He sees the lily as an object of great beauty. To Him, the humble lily was far more delightful than anything even the richest man on the earth could fashion.

The tender and gentle maiden realizes her lowly estate, but her beloved shepherd perceives her pure and humble life as the loveliest of all the other young maidens; she truly is a magnificent lily among the thorns.

Shulamite
*"3) As an apple-tree among the wild trees, So is my beloved among the youths. I delight to sit beneath its shade. For delicious is its fruit to my taste. 4) He led me into that **bower of delight**, And overshaded me with love"* (Sgs 2:3-4 – CDG).

The young maiden continues describing her beloved shepherd as a fruit-bearing tree, providing her with much-needed shade in the heat of the day. The Shulamite continues using eloquent metaphors, describing how he provides sweet nourishment in the form of delicious fruit symbolic of his love.

She then refers back to the secluded bower where they would meet (Sgs 1[17]), describing it as *"that bower of delight."* Merely thinking about their private retreat gives her an overwhelming longing for his protection and love. Feeling almost delirious in his absence she cries out:

> *"Oh, strengthen me with grape-cakes, Refresh me with apples,*
> ***For I am sick with love"*** (Sgs 2:5 – CDG).

Grape-cakes were made by baking pressed grapes in a delicious cake, and along with the apples, figuratively speak of the delightful love her beloved shepherd supplies. His love fills her heart with such tenderness that she feels weak without him near.

> *"Let his left hand be under my head*
> *And his right hand embrace me"* (Sgs 2:6 – NAS).

As the young maiden finishes describing how she is full of love for her beloved shepherd, she can barely hold her head up, and only wishes he were present. She longs to be reunited with the one whom her soul loves (Sgs 1[7]) and yearns for his presence to hold her in his arms in a passionate embrace.

All of this powerfully speaks of the love the believer feels toward the good Shepherd who is the lover of our soul. He provides us with a love that fills our hearts. While we have His wonderful Word to comfort and protect us during our sojourn in this life, we long to be reunited with Him when He returns.

The Shulamite is seen residing in the king's royal tent,

separated from her lover. She is tested and tempted by the court ladies and the king to turn her affections from her beloved. The believer is betrothed to the good Shepherd; however, the world attempts to lead us astray from a pure and sincere devotion to Him (*cf.* 2Co 11:2-3). The young maiden longs to be reunited with her beloved shepherd just as we long to be reunited with our Bridegroom.

> *"I charge you, O daughters of Jerusalem,*
> *By the gazelles or by the does of the field,*
> *Do not stir up nor awaken love*
> *Until it pleases."*
> (Sgs 2:7 – NKJV)

The Shulamite concludes her first soliloquy with the first of three admonitions to the court ladies (*cf.* Sgs 3:5, 8:4). They are attempting to provoke her affections toward the king who employs flatteries and enticing offers to try to win her love. The young maiden warns the court ladies not to interfere by trying to persuade her to give her heart to the king. She is espoused to another, and their love is still in bloom. To her, their love is a most wonderful gift that she honors and cherishes in her heart. She desires to give herself to her lover, and until it has been consummated, their attempt to rouse her passions is against the virtuous principles she so highly values.

In a similar manner, the believer is espoused to the good Shepherd and we are waiting for our great wedding day when our Bridegroom returns for us. In the meantime, the culture in which we live continuously attempts to seduce us, seeking to arouse our love for the things of this world. The Shulamite's warning to the court ladies, not to awaken love before its time, is a good example to remind us not to allow those who try to lead us away from the righteous path (Mat 6:33). Our hearts belong to Him, and until we see Him face to face (*cf.* Rev 22:4, Mat 5:8), we must not allow the "*court ladies and the kings*" of this world to turn our love away from our beloved Shepherd.

Act 2 – Longing During Separation

Shulamite longs to be reunited with her beloved.
(Song of Songs 2:8-17)

Scene 1 (2^{8-17})
(Shulamite maiden and court ladies in Solomon's royal tent.)
The second act continues with the young maiden before the court ladies in the king's country residence.

This scene represents a flashback in which the Shulamite reminiscences a previous visit her beloved shepherd once paid her in the springtime, inviting her to join him in the fields near her rustic home. Her brothers overheard their conversation and intervened.

Shulamite
*"8) The voice of my beloved! behold, he cometh leaping upon the mountains, skipping upon the hills. 9) My beloved is like a roe or a young hart: behold, he **standeth behind our wall**, he looketh forth at the windows, **shewing himself through the lattice**"* (Sgs 2:8-9).

The Shepherd
*"10) My beloved spake, and said unto me, **Rise up, my love, my fair one, and come away.**"*
(Sgs 2:10)

Literal Story
The young maiden is recollecting the time when her beloved shepherd visited her residence. His home was located nearby; however, he had to traverse hilly terrain before he reached her. No doubt, when a young boy first falls in love he would travel as quickly as possible to see her. Once he reached her house, he came to a window covered in lattice, where he lovingly asks her to come join him in the beautiful outdoors.

As we will discover in the next few verses of her dialogue before the court ladies, the winter has past and the wonderful springtime has arrived. Her beloved shepherd wants her to come share time together in one of the most lovely and picturesque times of the year.

Figurative Significance
Christ is pictured overcoming all of the many hindrances and obstacles (hills and mountains) we face in this life as He quickly comes for His beloved. The believer is blessed to be loved by the One who conquered death and is able to help us in all of our daily trials and temptations. Once he arrives, there is a wall that separates him from her, which brings to mind the door Christ is seen knocking on when He described the believers in Rev 3:20. This speaks to Jesus' desire to enter our life to enjoy intimate fellowship with us. But more than this, **He wants us to *come away with Him*,** and not to allow anything to come between us.

Jesus called out His disciples to leave their old way of life behind and to follow Him (Mar 1:17). Here He is inviting us to *come away with Him*, to abandon our old life and our own will, and allow Him to be our beloved Shepherd. He wants us to totally trust our life to His loving care. **Every new day** of our life He is calling each of His own to *come away with Him* and to permit Him total access to every area of our hearts and lives.

Prophetic Importance
Jesus Christ is finalizing the plans on our heavenly dwelling places and will return for His faithful beloved in the very near future (*cf.* Jhn 14:1-3, 23, Rev 14:1-5). In this beautiful story of love, our beloved Shepherd is calling out to His devoted bride to be prepared for the glorious time when He will return. Here He is crying out for us to get ready, to rise up from all earthly matters or concerns, and ensure that our wedding dress is spotless, without any wrinkle or blemish (Eph 5:26-27), and to allow Him to sanctify our lives by being immersed in His Word.

As we will discover in the next few acts of this captivating drama, the Beloved's return will disclose two distinctive types of maidens with divergent responses to His urgent plea.

Shulamite
(Continues describing her beloved shepherd's dialogue)

"11) For, lo, the winter is past, the rain is over and gone;
12) The flowers appear on the earth; the time of the singing of
birds is come, and the voice of the turtle is heard in our land;
*13) The **fig tree putteth forth her green figs**, and the vines with*
the tender grape give a good smell.
Arise, my love, my fair one, and come away."
(Sgs 2:11-13)

Literal Story
The Shulamite resumes relaying the details of her encounter with her beloved shepherd, telling us the time of the year when he came to visit her. Using the most charming terms, he describes the spring as a most enchanting and delightful time of the year. The rainy days of winter have past and the flowers are beginning to bloom, yielding a beautiful fragrance and color over the lush landscape. The birds, including the turtle-dove, fill the air with pleasant melodies; bidding the young maiden to come out and enjoy an exquisite time with her lover. His visit took place in the early spring, probably in mid-to-late March, since this is the time of year for the green figs to appear, and when the grapevines begin to blossom.[1]

Growing impatient in her delay to join him, the young shepherd again dearly asks his "dove" to come away from her sheltered room so he may behold her beauty and listen to her sweet voice:

"O my dove, that art in the clefts of the rock, in the secret
places of the stairs, let me see thy countenance, let me hear thy
voice; for sweet is thy voice, and thy countenance is comely."
(Sgs 2:14)

Figurative Significance
The beloved asks his lovely bride, a second time, to come away
and then asks to hear her voice. This speaks of the cry of our
Beloved's heart for us to come to that *secret place* where we
can experience intimate fellowship with Him (Mat 6:6). Our
beloved Shepherd is entreating us repeatedly to come away to
spend time with Him. "May the Lord's people avail themselves
of this rich and satisfying provision, this hiding place in the
deep sweet heart of His love!" (McPhee, p. 43). The devoted
bride longs to spend time alone with her beloved Shepherd.

Prophetic Importance
Written nearly 3,000 years ago, this beautiful story of love and
faithfulness has concealed one of the most anticipated and
glorious events since the resurrection of Christ. In one of His
last teachings before He left our planet He gave the following
parable:

> *"32) Now learn a **parable of the fig tree**;*
> *When his branch is yet tender, and putteth forth leaves,*
> *ye know that summer is nigh:*
> *33) So likewise ye, when ye shall see all these things,*
> ***know that it is near, even at the doors**.*
> *34) Verily I say unto you,*
> ***This generation shall not pass**,*
> *till all these things be fulfilled."*
> (Mat 24:32-34)

The rebirth of the nation of Israel in May 1948 represented the
budding of the fig tree (*cf.* Hsa 9:10, Joe 1:6-7). Jesus is telling
us that the generation that is alive to witness this event will not
pass away before He returns. In the Song of Songs, our beloved
Shepherd is calling His faithful to come away with Him at the
time when we see the fig tree begin to bud: "*putteth forth her
green figs*" (Sgs 2^{13}). The wonderful Shepherd and lover of our
souls, is telling us that He is coming for His faithful, devoted
bride sometime during the generation[2] that is alive today.

Immediately following the allusion to the formation of the nation of Israel, with the budding of the fig tree, the Song refers to the dove nestling in the rocks and cliffs (Sgs 2^{14}). This has a double prophetic application. First, it alludes to the first phase of His return for His awaiting bride, with our beloved Shepherd taking His beloved away to be with Him in the rapture; thereby allowing His lovely bride to find refuge in Christ (the Rock of ages). The second segment is a reference to the prophecy of Moab (see Jer 48:28). Moab generally typifies the world that opposes God, and this portion of the prophecy refers to the time during the tribulation period when God pours out His wrath on the earth, causing impenitent men to seek shelter in the rocks and caves[3] (*cf.* Hsa 10: 8, Luk 23:30, Rev 6:15-16).

After the young shepherd repeats his request for his beloved maiden to come join him in the fields, the Shulamite's brothers (who overheard their conversation) immediately intervene to prevent their meeting. The young maiden then informs the court ladies why her brothers forced her to go to work in the family's vineyards:

The Brothers of the Shulamite
"Catch us the foxes, the little foxes which destroy the vineyards,
For our vineyards are in bloom" (Sgs 2:15 – CDG).

When the young maiden first met the court ladies, she told them the reason for her dark complexion was because her brothers made her work in the hot sun (Sgs 1^{5-6}). While they were concerned for the family's livelihood, they were even more worried for their sister's virtue. Keeping her busy watching over their fields would also keep her from her lover. Her service in the vineyards would keep the little foxes from destroying the tender vines, and prevent them from digging holes in the soil, spoiling the roots. This important work would also protect their sister's reputation, by keeping her occupied during the daytime hours, away from her shepherd lover.

The little foxes figuratively speak to the little things that the believer can easily become beset with (*cf.* Heb 12:1), preventing our spiritual growth into maturity. These things may be little sins, habits, false teachings, or other hindrances in our lives that keep us from developing the abundant life He desires for us.

> *"The thief cometh not, but for to steal, and to kill, and to destroy: I am come that they might have life, and that they might have it more abundantly"* (Jhn 10:10).

Shulamite
"16) [She said distinctly] **My beloved is mine and I am his!** *He pastures his flocks among the lilies.*
17 [Then, longingly addressing her absent shepherd, she cried] Until the day breaks and the shadows flee away, **return hastily, O my beloved,** *and be like a gazelle or a young hart as you cover the mountains [which separate us]."*
(Sgs 2:16-17– AMP)

While the young maiden's brothers have prevented her from seeing her beloved shepherd at this time, she reiterates with steadfast assurance that she has given her heart to him and that he has the same conviction in his heart towards her.

Notice that she makes it abundantly clear that the one whom she loves is a shepherd for he *"pastures his flocks among the lilies,"* which certainly does not describe the king.

Realizing they have been temporarily separated by her brothers, she cried out for him to return in the evening (when *"the shadows flee away"*[4]), even though he would again be required to cross the hilly terrain that separated them.

The Shulamite concludes this act by telling us that she and her beloved shepherd are united in their love for one another, and she longs for him to return as quickly as possible.

Act 3 – Dream for Soulmate

Shulamite dreams of being with her beloved shepherd.
(Song of Songs 3:1-5)

> ## Scene 1 (3^{1-5})
> (Shulamite maiden in Solomon's royal tent in the country.)
>
> This scene represents a dream the Shulamite had, perhaps the first night she spent in the king's country retreat.
>
> Even though the court ladies and the king have attempted to turn her heart away from him, the young maiden's thoughts return to her beloved shepherd, even in her dreams.

Shulamite
*"1)...**By night on my bed I sought the one I love;**
I sought him, but I did not find him.
2) 'I will rise now,' I said, 'And go about the city; In the streets
and in the squares **I will seek the one I love.'**
I sought him, but I did not find him.
3) The watchmen who go about the city found me;
I said, 'Have you seen the one I love?'
4) Scarcely had I passed by them,*
**When I found the one I love. I held him and would not let
him go,** *Until I had brought him to the house of my mother,
And into the chamber of her who conceived me.
5) I charge you, O daughters of Jerusalem, By the gazelles or
by the does of the field,* **Do not stir up nor awaken love
Until it pleases**" (Sgs 3:1-5 – NKJV).

This is the first of two important dreams the young maiden has while residing in the king's residence. Both of these highly significant dreams hold valuable insight into the feelings and emotions she has towards her beloved shepherd, as well as very crucial prophetic implications for all believers living in these final days before our Beloved returns for His faithful, devoted bride.

Literal Story

The young maiden's heart is so devoted to her shepherd lover that she is thinking of being with him, even while she is sleeping. In this first dream she goes out into the streets trying to find her beloved. In her frantic search, she runs into watchmen on the streets and asks them if they have seen him. A short time later, she ecstatically finds him, and embraces him so tightly, for fear of ever being separated from him again. She then took him to her mother's home, which is the common practice for unmarried maidens planning to be married (*cf.* Gen 24:28, Rth 1:8), revealing her intent to consummate the relationship with her beloved shepherd, even in her dreams.

Figurative Significance

This first of two dreams the young maiden has while residing in the king's residence (away from her home) speaks to the believer's desire for personal fellowship with the Lord during our sojourn in this life. Once a person experiences a personal encounter with Christ, our spiritual life is **justified** by faith through the blood of His sacrificial death and resurrection. As we live out our daily life in Christ, we undergo periods of intimate fellowship with the Lord, as well as seasons when we feel He has abandoned us. God uses these times of His seeming absence as a means of **sanctifying** our souls, in order to test and try our faith, and to transform us to be more and more like Jesus as we allow Him to reign in our life.

In this dream, the believer earnestly seeks the Lord (*"him whom my soul loveth"* Sgs 3:2) with all diligence. This pictures one who seeks intimate fellowship with Christ by conscientiously searching out the Scriptures (Psa 119:105, Luk 15:8), allowing the Holy Spirit to speak to our hearts through prayer and meditation. When we do this with all earnestness, we can sense

His presence and the joy of finding His loving comfort, as promised by His word:

*"And the LORD, He is the One who goes before you. He will be with you, **He will not leave you nor forsake you**; do not fear nor be dismayed"* (Deu 31:8 – NKJV).

*"**And ye shall seek me, and find me,** **when ye shall search for me with all your heart**"* (Jer 29:13).

Whenever we may feel like the Lord has abandoned us, we have His assurance this will never happen. The Shulamite's first dream (while her beloved shepherd is absent) teaches us to diligently seek Him with all of our heart. When we do, we will be rewarded with His presence, both now in this life, as well as the glorious time when we join Him for our wedding (Rev 19:7-8). Our wedding day is pictured by the maiden being brought into the *"chamber"* of her mother's house, which is where the marriage is consummated (Gen 24:67, Mat 25:1-10), an allusion to the time we will be **glorified** as His bride.

Prophetic Importance
The Song of Solomon recorded an important prophecy that has been veiled within its poetic imagery for close to 3,000 years. Many noted commentators have explained that a great deal of the Song's narrative is conveyed to us in the form of parables. When Jesus walked the earth, he frequently taught His disciples the deeper teachings concerning the coming Kingdom through the use of parables (*cf.* Mat 13:10-15, Mar 4:10-12, Luk 8:9-10). Jesus used parables because they were meant to convey mysteries or secret knowledge regarding the kingdom of heaven, which only His disciples had eyes to see and ears to hear. They could hear and understand what Jesus was telling them because the disciple's hearts were not callous and hardened, as the skeptics and the religious leaders were.

Right before Christ was about to be crucified, He provided us with one of the most comprehensive teachings concerning God's future plans for mankind when Jesus returns. The Olivet Discourse has been widely interpreted by Bible scholars and teachers; however, what many students of the Scriptures fail to notice is that Christ was giving us an important prophecy for all of mankind living at the time of His return.

In order to understand the Olivet Discourse, it needs to be properly divided (2Ti 2:15) into the three distinctive groups of people Jesus discusses: the Jews, the Church, and the Gentiles[1]. The Church section of Christ's teaching can easily be distinguished because He used parables throughout this section. The first parable Jesus gave regarding the fig tree (Mat 24:32-34) tells us the general time of His return as previously described in Act 2 (p. 28). Later on, Jesus taught His disciples the parable of the ten virgins (Mat 25:1-13), which is described in Appendix 4. This parable shows there are two different types of believers, the wise and the foolish virgins.

While Christ's parable tells us believers fall into two different types of followers, the Song of Songs essentially recorded these two distinguishing types of believers in two unique prophetic dreams. In this **first dream**, the Shulamite describes the first type of believer, i.e., the **wise virgins** in Christ's prophetic parable. As we will discover when we reach Act 5, the Shulamite's **second dream** describes the second type of believer, the **foolish virgins** in His teaching.

5 Wise Virgins

In the young maiden's first dream she is lying on her bed at night and seeking her beloved. Even while sleeping, her constant thoughts are on him. She loves him so much that her only desire is to find him so she can be with him. The Shulamite then diligently tries to find her lover by seeking him throughout the city. Her painstaking and relentless search for her beloved allows her to find and embrace him – never to be separated again. Her lovely story of devotion and faithfulness is clearly pictured in the parable of the wise virgins.

The wise virgins have their lamps, along with an extra supply of oil in their jars, to keep their lamps burning brightly. They love their espoused with all of their hearts and are eagerly longing for the Bridegroom to return because their only desire is to be with Him when He returns. Because they are ready and properly prepared, they go into the wedding when He returns for them.

The Shulamite's allusion to the wise virgins is also typified by the faithful church of Philadelphia (Rev 3:7-13). The book of Revelation describes seven churches, and the church of Philadelphia stands out as the one most admired by Jesus. The members of this church are faithful believers who keep God's word. Even though they have little strength, they are loyal followers who exhibit Christ in their daily walk. Because of their faithfulness and obedience, they are given the wonderful promise by the Lord of being kept from the coming tribulation period and being pillars in God's temple (*cf.* Rev 3:10,12).

The Shulamite's longing and diligent search for her beloved finally paid off. Her heart is devoted to him and her life and faithfulness to her beloved shepherd is ultimately rewarded. This first dream that she had in her diligent search for her beloved shepherd is a prophetic picture of believers who love Jesus with all their hearts and are ready and eager to go away with our beloved Shepherd when He returns for us.

Concluding Admonition
*"I charge you, O daughters of Jerusalem... **Do not stir up nor awaken love Until it pleases**"* (Sgs 3:5 – NKJV).

Once the young maiden finishes telling the court ladies of her dream of searching for and finding her beloved shepherd, she reminds them again (*cf.* Sgs 2:7) that a person's love for another is a beautiful thing that must not be interfered with. They are attempting to turn her affections toward the king, which is a prophetic picture of others trying to influence the believer's heart away from the beloved Shepherd. The believer is espoused to the Bridegroom who is about to return for His faithful, devoted bride. The foolish virgins, along with the world, have little interest in His return because their hearts are devoted to the temporal things of the earth.

Since the Shulamite is espoused to her shepherd lover, she warns the court ladies not to disturb her love for her shepherd. This is a prophetic warning to the foolish, not to give their heart to the wrong lover. The Bridegroom is getting ready to return for those who love Him with all their heart. There is still time to acquire the extra measure of oil that the wise virgins possess.

THE WISE VIRGINS
"They That Were Ready Went in with Him to the Marriage
and the Door Was Shut."
Matt. 25:10.

The above picture is from **The Second Coming of Christ**, by Clarence Larkin, p.17, © 1918-1922. Used with permission of the Rev. Clarence Larkin Estate, P.O. Box 334, Glenside, PA 19038, U.S.A., 215-576-5590, www.larkinestate.com

Act 4 – Offer to Rescue

Her shepherd lover offers to rescue his Shulamite after she was taken to Solomon's royal palace in Jerusalem.
(Song of Songs 3:6 to 5:1)

Scene 1 (3^{6-11})
(Solomon's royal procession into Jerusalem.)

This scene pictures King Solomon returning from his northern country retreat as he enters the city of Jerusalem. This royal pageant is meant to dazzle the young maiden with all the pomp and splendor he is offering her if she becomes his bride.

Inhabitants of Jerusalem
"6) What is this coming up from the wilderness Like columns of smoke, Perfumed with myrrh and frankincense,
With all scented powders of the merchant?
7) Behold, it is the traveling couch of Solomon;
Sixty mighty men around it, Of the mighty men of Israel.
8) All of them are wielders of the sword, Expert in war;
Each man has his sword at his side,
Guarding against the terrors of the night."
(Sgs 3:6-8 – NAS)

In quite a dramatic manner, the Song's scenery now changes from the royal retreat in the country, as the inhabitants of Jerusalem gather to observe Solomon and his entourage approaching the city. This royal spectacle was an extravagant display of the king's luxurious lifestyle and wealth. The royal tent has been taken down as the king travels home to Jerusalem. The young maiden accompanies the king, as he rides in his traveling carriage, safely protected from all possible harm with sixty valiant armed guards to watch over and keep them safe.

Expensive and aromatic incense and spices fill the atmosphere with smoke and fragrant odors as the Shulamite maiden experiences a majestic ride from her home in the country to Solomon's stately kingdom. The magnificent splendor of this scene is a striking display of the pomp and opulence the king offers her. This regal parade is another attempt to seduce the young maiden away from her life with the lowly shepherd.

"9) King Solomon made himself a chariot of the wood of Lebanon. 10) He made the pillars thereof of silver, the bottom thereof of gold, the covering of it of purple, the midst thereof being paved with love, for the daughters of Jerusalem.
11) Go forth, O ye daughters of Zion,
and behold king Solomon with the crown wherewith his mother crowned him in the day of his espousals, and in the day of the gladness of his heart" (Sgs 3:9-11).

The inhabitants of Jerusalem continue describing the carriage, revealing just how truly lavish it is. It was fashioned from cedar and cypress woods, overlaid in gold with silver pillars supporting its canopy, which the court ladies adorned with material of "costly tapestry...spread over the purple cushion."[1] The rich and extravagant lifestyle the king maintained certainly would be appealing to any maiden offered such an opportunity. Riding in such a procession into the city of Jerusalem surely was a daunting experience for the humble country girl.

The king is pictured wearing the wedding crown that his mother made for him on a previous wedding day (Harper p. 24, Provan p. 305). Ginsburg astutely noted, "The design of Solomon in putting on this crown is evidently to dazzle the rustic girl" (Ginsburg p. 153). The king is trying to allure the vulnerable, young maiden by a royal entrance into his capital city, showing her the life of wealth and power he commands. This grand display was designed to overwhelm her with all the finer things in life that he is able to provide because of his position as king.

Similarly, the believer's sojourn in this life is constantly being enticed by the glamorous things of our modern culture. The material pleasures and trinkets of this world can easily distract us into believing these temporal things are important. While they may hold a certain degree of attractiveness for a season, their lasting value will soon fade away, leaving us empty and unfulfilled. The king is offering the young maiden a life beyond anything she could ever imagine – like winning the lottery in today's vernacular. As she enters the center of Solomon's world, she will be faced with one of her most challenging tests as he attempts to win her heart.

Scene 2 (4^{1-16} to 5^1)
(Shepherd with Shulamite in Jerusalem.)

The young shepherd lover has followed his Shulamite maiden on her journey to King Solomon's residence in the city of Jerusalem.

The young maiden invites the young shepherd into her room in the palace where he immediately begins to address her.

The Shepherd
*"1) **How fair you are, my love** [he said]**, how very fair!** Your **eyes** behind your veil [remind me] **of those of a dove;** your **hair** [makes me think of the black, wavy fleece] of a flock of [the Arabian] goats which one sees trailing down Mount Gilead 2) Your **teeth** are like a flock of shorn ewes which have come up from the washing, of which all are in pairs, and none is missing among them. 3) Your **lips** are like a thread of scarlet, and your mouth is lovely. Your **cheeks** are like halves of a pomegranate behind your veil. 4) Your **neck** is like the tower of David, built for an arsenal, whereon hang a thousand bucklers, all of them shields of warriors. 5) Your two **breasts** are like two fawns, like twins of a gazelle that feed among the lilies."*
(Sgs 4:1-5 – AMP)

> Practically all commentators see this address to the young maiden as being made by King Solomon. Fortunately, Ginsberg adeptly noted that the king does not make his entrance here, but he chooses to make his appearance at a more important time. We will discover the strategic timing of King Solomon's entrances when we reach Act 6.

The young shepherd had closely followed his lovely maiden on her four-day journey from Solomon's summer retreat over 50 miles north of Jerusalem. He was so in love with her that he probably did not let the king's royal train out of his sight, looking for the opportune time to speak with her. The Shulamite is now residing in one of the rooms in the king's lavish palace where the young shepherd addresses his beloved.

For further proof that this is the shepherd speaking, he commences by using almost the exact description he had used on one of the occasions when they first met (see p. 20):

"Behold, you are beautiful, my love! Behold, you are beautiful!
You have doves' eyes*"* (Sgs 1:15 – AMP).

After starting with her eyes, he continues to focus primarily on her face by using beautiful metaphors describing her stunning beauty. Ginsberg eloquently depicts the beloved shepherd's simile of her hair "like a flock of goats, i.e. the tresses, dangling from the crown of her head, are as beautiful as Mount Gilead covered with the shaggy herd. The hair of goats is exceedingly delicate, soft (Gen 27:16), long, and black (1Sa 19:13); and when the sun shines upon it, reflects such a glare that the eye can hardly bear the luster....Nothing, therefore, could more beautifully express the curly hair of a woman, dangling down from the crown of her head, than the sight, at a distance, of a flock of goats running down from the summit of this verdant hill on a beautiful day" (Ginsburg p. 154).

The shepherd continues describing her lovely face, noting her perfectly aligned white teeth, which glimmer against her moist crimson colored lips, nestled between her full, rosy red cheeks. Her attractive, veiled face merges with her elegant neck, which is adorned with numerous necklaces that he compares to warrior's shields used to decorate the walls of David's strong tower. He then compares her two breasts to a pair of fawns (gazelles or deer), which are seen grazing in a beautiful pasture filled with delightful lilies (*cf.* Pro 5:18-19 & Burrowes, p. 358).

The shepherd's eloquent portrayal of her exquisite beauty is interrupted by the Shulamite's excited reply:

Shulamite
"Until the cool of the day When the shadows flee away,
I will go my way to the mountain of myrrh
And to the hill of frankincense" (Sgs 4:6 – NAS).

Here, she is expressing her desire to leave that very evening to meet him in the hilly countryside, fragrant with lush foliage away from the king's stately residence. She is so elated to see her shepherd lover after being separated from him; she wants to immediately run away to be with him.

The Shepherd
"7) You are altogether beautiful, my love; **there is no flaw in you.** *8)* **Come with me** *from Lebanon,* **my bride; come with me** *from Lebanon.* **Depart from** *the peak of Amana, from the peak of Senir and Hermon,*
from the dens of lions, from the mountains of leopards.
9) You have **captivated my heart,** *my sister,* **my bride;** *you have* **captivated my heart** *with* **one glance of your eyes,** *with one jewel of your necklace"* [2] (Sgs 4:7-9 – ESV).

Emboldened by her encouragement, he offers to rescue her from the king's abode, which he metaphorically describes as a den of lions and mountain leopards that dwell in the unsafe and inaccessible mountain peaks found in Lebanon. His heart has been strengthened with the resolve to save her from the clutches of her hostile surroundings. His heart is captivated by her response, and he now possesses the courage to ask her to come away with him from the king's perilous kingdom.

Notice that the shepherd also identifies his Shulamite as his bride two times in the above verses. Before this scene is finished he will call her his bride four more times. She has been espoused to her shepherd, who is the "*one whom her soul loves*" (1^7), in much the same way that we as believers are espoused to our heavenly Bridegroom.

Also observe that the shepherd declares there is no flaw in her, which also symbolizes the bride of Christ as depicted by the Apostle Paul in describing her preparation for her glorious wedding day: "*...26) having cleansed her by the washing of water with the word, 27 so that he might present the church to himself in splendor, **without spot or wrinkle** or any such thing, that she might be **holy and without blemish**"* (Eph 5:26-27 – ESV). This pictures the beautiful bride who is without **any flaw** because she allows the Word of God to cleanse and sanctify her soul in order to be ready when the Bridegroom returns to take her to her true home. As the young shepherd is offering his lovely maiden to come away with him from Solomon's domain, our Shepherd is waiting for just the right time to come take His awaiting bride away from this foreign land that is not our home.

The shepherd then continues extolling the many wonderful virtues of his beloved:

The Shepherd
*"10) How beautiful is your love, my sister, **my bride**!*
How much better is your love than wine,
and the fragrance of your oils than any spice!

*11) Your lips drip nectar, **my bride**;*
honey and milk are under your tongue; the
fragrance of your garments is like the fragrance of Lebanon.
*12) A **garden locked** is my sister,*
***my bride**, a spring locked, **a fountain sealed**."*
(Sgs 4:10-12 – ESV)

We remember that the young maiden had previously begun her
soliloquy of her beloved by describing how her love for him
was better than wine (1^2). He now declares that his love for her
is also better than wine and that the fragrance of her perfume
along with the loving words that fall from her lips is like a drop
of honeycomb that fills his heart (*cf.* Pro 16:24).

The shepherd then uses another beautiful metaphor to describe
the purity and chastity of his beloved by stating that her garden
is locked and that her fountain is sealed. She is a pure virgin,
keeping herself for the one she loves. The Shulamite is indeed a
virtuous young maiden who will only belong to the one man she
chooses. This clearly speaks to the believer who has decided, in
a similar manner, that his or her heart only belongs to one
master. The world and others may attempt to seduce us, but we
have resolved to give our hearts to the Lord and to only follow
Him (Jos 24:15 and Mat 6:24).

The shepherd then concludes his depiction of his beloved:

*"13) **Your shoots** are an orchard of pomegranates with all*
choicest fruits, henna with nard,
14) nard and saffron, calamus and cinnamon, with all trees of
frankincense, myrrh and aloes, with all choice spices
*15) a **garden fountain, a well of living water**, and flowing*
streams from Lebanon.
16) Awake, O north wind, and come, O south wind! Blow upon
my garden, let its spices flow."
(Sgs 4:13-16 – ESV)

The young shepherd uses the picture of ***"shoots are an orchard,"*** perceiving their future union, which will bear the fruits of children (*cf.* Psa 128:3). Most young women desire to have children and her beloved's desire is to eventually be united with her for that very purpose. Unlike Solomon who wants her for his own pleasure, her beloved shepherd desires to join her in a sacred union that produces abundant, delightful fruits.

Shulamite
"Let my beloved come to his garden,
and eat its choicest fruits" (Sgs 4:16 – ESV).

Realizing they have the same desires, the young maiden is telling him that she longs for the time when they can be together again so she will become available to him and to him alone.

The Shepherd
*"1) I came to my garden, my sister, **my bride**, I gathered my myrrh with my spice, I ate my honeycomb with my honey, I drank my wine with my milk"* (Sgs 5:1^{a-d} – ESV).

Since the time for their wedding is in the future, the shepherd is declaring that after hearing her reply to his proposal he knows their hearts will soon be united when they are married.

Court Ladies
"Eat, friends, drink, and be drunk with love!"
(Sgs 5:1^e – ESV)

Witnessing the dialogue between the young lovers, and watching him hold her in a loving embrace, the court ladies now understand that the happy couple is deeply in love. Perceiving their wonderful joy, they encourage them to enjoy their happiness together.

Act 5 – Dream of Separation

Shulamite dreams again and tells the Daughters of Jerusalem about her dream of her shepherd lover.
(Song of Songs 5:2 to 5:8)

Scene 1 (5^{2-8})
(Shulamite's dream while residing in Jerusalem.)

After her young lover leaves her room, she goes to bed and dreams again of her beloved shepherd. Upon awakening, she tells the court ladies about her dream.

Shulamite

"2) I sleep, but my heart is awake; It is the voice of my beloved!
He knocks, saying, 'Open for me, my sister, my love, My dove,
my perfect one; For my head is covered with dew,
My locks with the drops of the night.'
*3) **I have taken off my robe;** How can I put it on again?*
I have washed my feet; How can I defile them?
4) My beloved put his hand By the latch of the door,
And my heart yearned for him.
5) I arose to open for my beloved, And my hands dripped with
myrrh, My fingers with liquid myrrh, On the handles of the lock.
6) I opened for my beloved,
But my beloved had turned away and was gone.
*My heart leaped up when he spoke. **I sought him, but I could***
***not find him;** I called him, but he gave me no answer.*
7) The watchmen who went about the city found me.
They struck me, they wounded me; The keepers of the walls
Took my veil away from me."
(Sgs 5:2-7 – NKJV)

This is the second of two highly significant dreams the young maiden experiences while sleeping in the king's royal residence.

Readers may want to review the first dream (Act 3, pp. 31-36), since this second dream contrasts the first one in several very significant ways. As we will discover, this second dream holds vital prophetic importance for believers in these last days, as we await the return of our beloved Shepherd.

Literal Story
In this second dream, the young maiden hears her beloved shepherd knocking on the door, because he wants to come inside with her. The Shulamite does not come to open the door, giving the excuse that she had already gone to bed for the evening, having washed her feet and taken off her garment. After her beloved had withdrawn his hand from the door, she anxiously got out of bed to open the door. Once she finally opened it, her beloved had withdrawn, and he was gone! She then frantically goes out searching for her young shepherd, but this time the watchmen who guard the city streets hurt her and take her garment away (apparently because they had mistaken her to be a woman of the streets (Duguid, p. 128).

Figurative Significance
Unlike the first dream, where the young maiden immediately searched for her beloved: *"him whom my soul loveth"* (Sgs 3:2), in this second dream she immediately gives excuses why she does not want to even get out of bed to go to the door. This pictures the believer who is preoccupied with his or her own self interest. These types of believers are more concerned for their own ease and comfort, unwilling to even take the necessary time to cloth themselves. This pictures the believer who fails to *"study to shew thyself approved unto God, a workman that needeth not to be ashamed, rightly dividing the word of truth"* (2Ti 2:15). By not spending time reading and studying the Word of God, this believer lacks the necessary acquaintance with spiritual matters, and may be ashamed one day if he or she fails to awaken from their slumber. As pointed out by Hudson Taylor, "It was her condition of self-satisfaction

and love of ease that closed the door…[being] more occupied with her own graces than with His desires" (Taylor, pp. 44-46).

This is in stark contrast to the believer pictured by the young Shulamite's first dream (see p. 32) where the diligent searching of the Scriptures produced intimate fellowship with the Lord, leading to a life that is prepared and eager for the time when Christ calls us to our grand wedding day. The believer typified by the Shulamite's first dream is a picture of the bride of Christ who is diligently in the process of preparing her garment for her wedding so she will be dressed and ready for her beloved Shepherd when they are joined together on their wedding day (see Psa 45:13-15, Mat 25:10, Eph 5:26-27, Rev 19:7-8).

The believer typified in this second dream is the exact opposite. The cares of Christ take secondary importance to this Christian. Instead of allowing the Holy Spirit to lead his or her life, with Jesus guiding and directing them, their flesh has not been crucified (Gal 2:20), allowing worldly cares and carnal desires to dominate. Instead of preparing her own wedding garment as depicted by the bride, this believer is pictured as undressed and unprepared when the beloved knocks on her door.

Prophetic Importance
As previously described in our review of the Shulamite's first dream, much of the Song of Solomon is written in the form of parables. Christ used parables to teach His disciples mysteries and secret knowledge concerning the kingdom of heaven. In His parable of the ten virgins (Mat 25:1-13), he shows us there are two different types of believers, the wise and foolish virgins. While Christ's parable tells us believers fall into two different types of followers, the Song of Songs essentially recorded these two distinguishing types of believers in two unique prophetic dreams. We discovered that in the Shulamite's **first dream** she vividly represents the first type of believer, i.e., the **wise virgins** in Christ's prophetic parable.

Here in the Shulamite's **second dream** we will learn how the Song of Songs prophetically describes the second type of believer, the **foolish virgins** in our Lord's important teaching.

5 Foolish Virgins

In the young maiden's second dream she hears her beloved shepherd knocking on the door. This scene is pictured by the Apostle John when he saw Christ seeking entrance into the believer's lives, epitomized by the church of Laodicea:

*"Behold, **I stand at the door and knock**.*
If anyone hears My voice and opens the door, I will come in to
him and dine with him, and he with Me" (Rev 3:20 – NKJV).

Prominent biblical scholar Gregory K. Beale wisely noted regarding Sgs 5^2, that Christ is "always standing at the doors of the hearts of those believers who have become cold in their love and enmeshed in the pursuit of what the world has to offer." Professor Beal also perceived, "The description of the church of Laodicea is probably uncomfortably close to the situation of the church in our culture" (Beale, p. 93). The Shulamite's second dream is a depiction of the lukewarm church of Laodicea (Rev 3:14-22), which represents the modern church of today. Believers living in these end times will want to pay close attention to the prophetic meaning in this Song's second dream.

The church of Laodicea is lukewarm and about to be spit out of His mouth because Jesus views them as: *"wretched, and miserable, and poor, and blind, and **naked**"* (*cf.* Rev 3:16-17). Believers found in this church have deceived themselves into thinking they are model Christians, however, Christ finds them to be the exact opposite. Notice that He says they are *"**naked**."* While these believers have obtained their robe of righteousness provided by Christ, Jesus says that they are naked because they have not been preparing their wedding garment of fine linen as typified in the Shulamite's first dream discussed above (p. 47).

In this second dream, the Shulamite does not even bother to get out of bed to open the door for her beloved shepherd because she is already **undressed** and unwilling to put her garment back on to open the door! This is an allusion to lukewarm and slothful believers who are more concerned with their own desires and comfort than living to please Christ. The young maiden was **naked** and unprepared when her beloved arrived, and when she finally arose, it was too late; he had already gone.

This second dream represents a prophetic picture of the foolish virgins in our Lord's parable of the ten virgins (Mat 25:1-13). The foolish virgins had their lamps, but they failed to obtain their extra oil to keep their lamps burning. They wanted to borrow some oil from the wise virgins, but their lethargy in providing for their own supply resulted in them being turned away when the Bridegroom arrived. Similarly, the laziness of the young maiden caused her to miss the chance to be with her beloved, a picture of the foolish virgins being shut out.[1]

THE FOOLISH VIRGINS
"Too Late! Too Late! Ye Cannot Enter Now."

Prophetic Warning and Admonition
The young maiden's second dream represents a prophetic warning to believers, particularly during these final days of the church age. While the believers alluded to in her first dream were diligently seeking, and in love with the beloved Shepherd, the believers depicted in her second dream are undressed and about to fall asleep. This symbolizes the lukewarm believers being shut out when the Bridegroom returns for His faithful and wise followers who are longing for Him to return.

The picture of believers being shut out is further alluded to in the Shulamite's second dream: *"6) **I sought him, but I could not find him**; I called him, but he gave me no answer. 7) The watchmen...found me. They struck me, they wounded me...Took my veil away from me"* (Sgs 5:6-7 – NKJV).

In this dream, the young maiden frantically looks for her beloved shepherd in vain, and while looking for him, she is seriously mistreated and hurt by the watchmen. This horrific experience by the Shulamite is a prophetic picture of the Lord's rebuke and chastening (*cf.* Pro 3:11-12 and Heb 12:5-6)[2] of Laodicean believers if they fail to repent before He returns:

> *"As many as I love, I **rebuke and chasten**:*
> ***be zealous** therefore, and **repent**"* (Rev 3:19).

God is calling us to be zealous for Him and for us to turn away from anything that displeases Him, forsaking all worldly or selfish interests while making it a top priority to yield our lives to His perfect will by earnestly seeking our beloved Shepherd.

Remorseful at being separated from her beloved shepherd, she admonishes the court ladies: *"That you tell him I am lovesick!"* (Sgs 5:8 – NKJV). This second dream is a wake-up call to all believers for how much our beloved Shepherd really does mean to us. We are desperately lovesick without Him and His love.

Act 6 – Longing for Her Lover

She tells the Daughters of Jerusalem all about her lover. Solomon tries to allure her to him (6:4-10 & 7:1-9). She refuses, stating that she is espoused to her beloved in the country.
(Song of Songs 5:9 to 8:4)

Scene 1 (5^9 to 6^3)
(Shulamite before the court ladies.)

After the young maiden recounts her dream, the court ladies ask her why her beloved shepherd is so special. She then tells the court ladies all of his endearing qualities.

Court Ladies
"What is your beloved More than another beloved,
O fairest among women? *What is your beloved More than another beloved, That you so charge us?"* (Sgs 5:9 – NKJV)

Having told the court ladies that she is lovesick without her beloved, they want to know what is so extraordinary about him, and why she is willing to give up all the king can offer, for him.

Shulamite
"10) My beloved is white and ruddy,
Chief among ten thousand.
*11) His **head** is like the finest gold;*
*His **locks** are wavy, And black as a raven.*
*12) His **eyes** are like doves By the rivers of waters,*
Washed with milk, And fitly set.
*13) His **cheeks** are like a bed of spices, Banks of scented herbs.*
*His **lips** are lilies, Dripping liquid myrrh.*
*14) His **hands** are rods of gold Set with beryl.*
*His **body** is carved ivory Inlaid with sapphires.*
*15) His **legs** are pillars of marble Set on bases of fine gold.*
*His **countenance** is like Lebanon, Excellent as the cedars.*

*16) His **mouth** is most sweet, Yes, **he is altogether lovely.**
This is my beloved, **And this is my friend,**
O daughters of Jerusalem!"* (Sgs 5:10-16 – NKJV)

The young maiden begins and ends her description of her lover by saying he is *"chief among ten thousand...and altogether lovely."* His distinguished radiance makes him stand out in a large crowd and he is the most desirable young man of all. More importantly, to her, her beloved shepherd is her closest friend. In between, her flattering account offers **ten** important features that captivate her. The number ten "signifies *the perfection of Divine order*...It implies that nothing is wanting."[1] To the young Shulamite her beloved is perfect!

When the young shepherd described the young maiden, their eyes were the only common feature depicted by the other. Significantly, they both viewed the other person's eyes as doves (*cf.* 1^{15} and 4^1). As noted earlier, the dove is a symbol of purity, innocence, and fidelity; qualities both parties radiate and which speaks to their kindred spirits and deep love for one another. Sharing the same emblem of *"eyes of doves,"* these young lovers are indeed true soulmates, inseparably linked in each other's heart. Their wholehearted attachment speaks to the believers forming the bride of Christ, who have hearts similarly devoted to their beloved Shepherd. Jesus is their best friend.

While some commentators attempt to show how these ten attributes of the young shepherd relate to features of our Lord, Hudson Taylor preferred to show the stark contrast between the young maiden's description and how Christ is portrayed in the Scriptures: "In Rev. 1, we see the Son of Man Himself...and His head and His hair were white as wool...but the bride sees her Bridegroom in all the vigor of youth, with locks 'bushy, and black as a raven.'"[2] While there are similarities and differences, this writing will not belabor them here. Suffice it to say, the Shulamite has answered the court ladies' query. He's her friend!

Court Ladies
*"Whither is thy beloved gone, **O thou fairest among women?**
Whither is thy beloved turned away?
Say, that we may seek him with thee?"*
(Sgs 6:1 – CDG)

Hearing such a magnificent account of her beloved, the court ladies then ask her (*cf.* 5[9]) where he had gone so they may help her look for him.

Shulamite
*"2) **My beloved has gone to his garden,** To the beds of spices,
To **feed his flock** in the gardens, And **to gather lilies**.
3) **I am my beloved's,** And **my beloved is mine. He feeds his
flock among the lilies**"* (Sgs 6:2-3 – NKJV).

The young maiden undeniably verifies, once again, that the person of whom she has given such a wonderful portrayal is a shepherd and could not be the king (*cf.* 2[16-17], see p. 30).

Scene 2 (6[4-13])
(Solomon enters with the Shulamite maiden and the court ladies.)

Having heard the young maiden speak of her beloved, the king comes forward in the attempt to win her heart.

King Solomon made his initial appearance before the young maiden the first time when he overheard her describing her shepherd lover to the court ladies (*cf.* 1[7-8], p. 17). Once again, he makes his entrance upon hearing her tell the court ladies about her beloved. The king strategically times his emergence before her, as he endeavors to lure her affections.

Solomon
*"4) You are as **beautiful as Tirzah** [capital of the northern
kingdom's first king], my love, and as **comely as Jerusalem,**
[but you are] as **terrible as a bannered host**!*

*5) **Turn away your** [flashing] **eyes** from me, **for they have
overcome me!** **Your hair** is like a flock of goats trailing down
from Mount Gilead. 6) **Your teeth** are like a flock of ewes
coming from their washing, of which all are in pairs, and not
one of them is missing. 7) **Your cheeks** are like halves of a
pomegranate behind your veil. 8) There are **sixty queens** and
eighty concubines, and virgins without number;
9) But my dove, my undefiled and perfect one, stands alone
[above them all]; she is the only one of her mother, she is the
choice one of her who bore her. The daughters saw her and
called her blessed and happy, yes, the queens and the
concubines, and they praised her."*
(Sgs 6:4-9 – AMP)

The king tells the young maiden that she is as beautiful as the
nation's first capital city in the north, as well as the majestic
beauty of Jerusalem (*cf.* Lam 2:15). Using the metaphor of *"a
bannered host,"* he is telling her that he is awe-struck at
beholding her beauty, as if one were caught spell-bound before
an army approaching with many banners. While the shepherd
said her eyes reminded him of those of a dove, the king is
overwhelmed by them. He is captivated by her. He then
describes her hair, teeth, and cheeks using practically identical
similes her shepherd lover had used (*cf.* 4¹⁻³).

The king then tells the young Shulamite that he currently has
more than one hundred and forty queens and concubines in his
harem. To him she is the most attractive of them all. She
stands far above every one of them.

*"10) Who is this who shines like the dawn – as beautiful
as the moon, bright as the sun,
awe-inspiring as an army with banners?"* (Sgs 6:10 – HCSB)

The king then reminisces of the time when the Shulamite first
came into his presence. The day she accidentally happened into

the king's view, while he was staying at his country residence, is a day he will never forget. Seeing her for the very first time that charming summer day will always be remembered by the king as the day the young maiden captured his heart.

By recalling that breathtaking day, the king hopes to evoke pleasant memories of their first encounter. He reminds her how he was dazzled by her exquisite charm. The young maiden remembers that fateful day and explains the circumstances of what happened:

Shulamite

"11) I went down to the nut orchard to look at the blossoms of the valley, to see whether the vines had budded, whether the pomegranates were in bloom.

12) Before I was aware, my desire set me among the chariots of my kinsman, a prince" (Sgs 6:11-12 – ESV).

She was simply visiting the orchard to gather fruits and nuts for her family, when she stumbled into the king's retreat, where she unwittingly came into the presence of the king.

After conveying her account, she begins to leave. Immediately, King Solomon asks her to come back:

Solomon

"13) Return, return, O Shulammite, return, return, that we may look upon you.

Shulamite

Why should you look upon the Shulammite?"

(Sgs 6:13[a-c] – ESV)

She humbly asks him what could he see in a mere rustic peasant girl? The king replies that observing her is like watching a joyful dance performed by double choirs of young maidens:[3]

Solomon

"...Like a dance to double choirs" (Sgs 6:13[d] – CDG).

The previous section of the Song of Songs is one of the most difficult and widely interpreted parts of the Song. As perceptively noted by Pope, "The meanings ascribed to the word, or the emendations [improve by critical editing] proposed, are inevitably dictated by theories of interpretation" (Pope, p. 595).

Since this writing takes the view that the Song is a love story that revolves around three primary characters: Solomon, the Shulamite maiden, and her shepherd lover, we largely follow Christian Ginsburg's understanding of this section. He observed: "that the Shulamite in her deeply rooted affections for her beloved shepherd is unmoved by all the persuasions, promises, and eulogies of Solomon and the courtiers, had just explained in the preceding verse how she came to be noticed and picked up by the king, and had started to leave. 'But the king entreated her to return, that he might look at her once more. The Shulamite, pausing a little, turns round and modestly asks: 'What will you behold in the Shulamite?' That is, what can you see in a humble rustic girl?" (Pope, p. 595).

Ginsburg goes on to explain Solomon's reply, "*Like a dance to double choirs,*" by stating: "to see thee is like gazing at the charming view of a festive choir expressing their merriment in a sacred dance. The Hebrews...used sacred dancing, accompanied by vocal and instrumental music, as expressive of joy and rejoicing (Exod. Xv. 20; Sam vi. 15; Ps. cxlix. 3). A sight of such an assemblage of various beauties, all swelling their voices into one song of joy, and blending their several forms in one choral dance of joy, must have afforded a delightful picture...therefore, does the captivated monarch compare the view of the Shulamite... to...a dance, the joyous dancing on a festive occasion" (Ginsburg, pp. 176-177).

Before we move on to the final scenes of Act 6, it is important to review some of the figurative implications and prophetic importance in the section we just examined. To help with this, Lyn Mize provided a more accurate translation of this passage of Scripture with the help of Keil and Delitzsch:

"10) Who is this who looks down like the dawn, **beautiful as the moon, pure as the sun, set up as the chief one?** *11) 'I had gone down to the orchard of nut trees to see the blossoms of the valley to see whether the vine had budded or the pomegranites had budded. 12) Before I knew what was happening,* **my soul set me upon the lead chariot of the princely people.'** *13) 'Return, return, O Shulamite!* **Return, return,** *that we may gaze upon you. What is so special about the Shulamite? To be placed in the company of the sacred courts.'"*[4]

Figurative and Prophetic Importance
So far in our analysis of the two dreams that the Shulamite shared, we have seen the two different types of believers typified in the Song: the faithful, virtuous, and devoted longing to be with their Shepherd lover, representing the bride of Christ; and the carnal, worldly, lukewarm who are not concerned or prepared for Christ's second coming. This distinction is clearly shown in the above verses. Verse 10 is a picture of the Shulamite who symbolizes the bride *"beautiful as the moon, pure as the sun, set up as the chief one,"* reflecting the glory of her beloved Shepherd (*cf.* Rev 1:16). Then in verse 12, *"she was enraptured as if she had been caught up in a royal chariot..."* (Duguid, p. 143), which is an allusion to the Lord catching His beloved away to be with Him in the rapture. After she is gone, those who watched her leave want her to return. They don't understand what is so special about her. This is a prophetic picture of the foolish virgins described in Act 5 and Appendix 4. As noted by Mize, "Four times she was beckoned by the people to return so they could look upon her to see what was so special about her....... In verse 13, the Hebrew word for

armies has a figurative meaning of *sacred court.*" While they are "calling for her return, so they could look at her in order to see what was so special about her; she was among the sacred court in the New Jerusalem with her Beloved."[4]

Combining the insight gleaned from Ginsburg and Mize, we can see a festive portrait of the bride of Christ joyously singing and dancing before their beloved Bridegroom in the sacred courts of the New Jerusalem. With much merriment and rejoicing, they praise their beloved Shepherd as they share a joyful and enchanted time together. What a glorious day that will be!

Scene 3 ($7^1$to 7^9)
(Solomon's final attempt to win the young maiden.)

The king continues in his endeavor to try to win her heart by offering her the most passionate and flattering praises of her lovely beauty.

Solomon

*"1) How beautiful are your sandaled **feet**, princess! The curves of your **thighs** are like jewelry, the handiwork of a master.*
*2) Your **navel** is a rounded bowl; it never lacks mixed wine.*
*Your **waist** is a mound of wheat surrounded by lilies.*
*3) Your **breasts** are like two fawns, twins of a gazelle.*
*4) Your **neck** is like a tower of ivory, your **eyes** like pools in Heshbonby the gate of Bath-rabbim. Your **nose** is like the tower of Lebanon looking toward Damascus.*
*5) Your **head** crowns you like Mount Carmel,*
*the **hair** of your head like purple cloth*
***a king** could be **held captive** in your tresses.*
6) How beautiful you are
and how pleasant, my love, with such delights!
7) Your stature is like a palm tree;
*your **breasts** are clusters of fruit.*
8) I said, 'I will climb the palm tree
and take hold of its fruit.'

*'May your **breasts** be like clusters of grapes,*
and the fragrance of your breath like apricots.
*9) Your **mouth** is like fine wine*
flowing smoothly for my love,[5]
gliding past my lips and teeth!"
(Sgs 7:1-9 – HCSB)

Remember that Solomon is attempting to convince the young maiden to turn her affections from the young shepherd. She was about ready to leave, when the king asked her to come back (Sgs 6:13). He is making one final effort in order to persuade her to stay with him instead.

The king proceeds to describe how beautiful the Shulamite is to him. He begins with her feet and moves up her gorgeous body, using some of the most erotic and explicit images found in the Song. When the young maiden was describing her shepherd lover she pointed out ten important features about him, signifying he is perfect in her eyes (see Sgs 5[10-16], p. 51). In describing the Shulamite, the king also gives ten significant characteristics about her, suggesting that he views her as a perfect catch to add to his harem. In saying, *"a king could be held captive in your tresses,"* he is undeniably telling her that he has been captivated by her beauty.

This brings to mind how the young shepherd told his beloved maiden that he was captivated with one glance of her eyes (see Sgs 4[9], p. 41). With just a glance from her beautiful eyes, his heart was captured. While the king was captivated by her lustrous, shimmering black hair; her young lover's heart was taken by her eyes, which linked the two together as true soulmates, as discussed earlier (*cf.* Sgs 1[15], 4[1], 5[12], see p. 52).

The king continues his flattering description of her attractive body by focusing on her lovely breasts, revealing his intentions are to *"climb the palm tree and take hold of its fruit."* This rather explicit metaphor requires very little explanation since its meaning is rather obvious. "Most commentators identify her breasts as the object of his grasping" (Carr, p.162), and one observed, "to climb the palm tree is to fertilize it. Solomon is using some contemporary language of the vineyard to say he intends to make love to Shulamith right away!" (Dillow, p. 136) It seems rather clear: the king wants the Shulamite for her body.

Solomon had previously attempted to lure her heart away from her shepherd lover by showing her the great wealth and power that he commands, which he is offering her (cf. Sgs 1^{9-11}, 3^{6-11}). His final approach, as he seeks to win her love, is to show her that she ranks the highest – the most attractive and leading maiden of all his numerous wives and concubines (Sgs 6^{4-9}) and now he tells her of his intense desire to make love with her. Possessing great charisma, charm, and a handsome physique, his final tactic is to offer her the opportunity to experience the pleasure he can provide her physically. The king's final attempt to win her heart is to seduce her by offering her sexual pleasure.

This considerable seduction by the king speaks to the tremendous seduction that the world makes against believers. In order to induce us to forsake our devotion and commitment to Christ, the world provides a constant stream of things aimed at seducing us. We live in a culture where believers are tempted by worldly pleasures provided by entertainment, the media, the internet, and the list goes on and on. Believers can become so desensitized that we forget that this world is not our true home. All the worldly wealth, power, and pleasure offered to us on a daily basis is only temporal (cf. 1Jo 2:15-17)[6].

Solomon is offering the Shulamite the chance to have everything he can provide. She can have it all, if she decides to give herself to him. Similarly, the world tries to seduce us into believing temporal things are important, when in fact, they can never satisfy the heart that is devoted to the good Shepherd.

Scene 4 (7^{10} to 8^4)
(Shulamite rejects Solomon in favor of her beloved shepherd.)

She refuses the king by telling him that her affections have already been pledged to her beloved shepherd lover. The king exits and her beloved joins her with the court ladies.

Shulamite
*"10) **I am my beloved's**, and his desire is toward me.*
*11) **Come, my beloved**, let us go forth into the field;*
let us lodge in the villages.
12) Let us get up early to the vineyards; let us see if the vine
flourish, whether the tender grape appear, and the
pomegranates bud forth: there will I give thee my loves.
13) The mandrakes give a smell, and at our gates are all
manner of pleasant fruits, new and old, which I have laid up for
*thee, **O my beloved**"* (Sgs 7:10-13).

The young maiden had previously been engaged to her beloved shepherd, and she now tells the king that she belongs to him. She had already pledged her heart and made a commitment to the love of her life. On hearing the Shulamite's reply, the king exits her room and the young maiden immediately invites her beloved to come into her room. She then invites her beloved to return with her to their place in the country where they will share their life together. While the king was offering her all the wealth, pleasure, and rank in his vast kingdom, the young maiden had promised her heart to her beloved shepherd.

The young maiden's decision is a superb depiction of virtue and faithfulness, providing believers with a precious example to apply to our lives. While the world may offer us many tempting allurements that may seem worthwhile, our hearts have already been pledged to our Beloved. Like the Shulamite, we need divine strength and wisdom to resist all worldly enticements, and to completely follow (Jos 24:15)[7] our beloved Shepherd.

"1) If only I could treat you like my brother, one who nursed at my mother's breasts, I would find you in public and kiss you, and no one would scorn me.
2) I would lead you, I would take you, to the house of my mother who taught me. I would give you spiced wine to drink from my pomegranate juice" (Sgs 8:1-2 – HCSB).

The Shulamite's thoughts turn to her desire to return home, but she realizes that she will not be able to openly display her love toward her beloved. She wishes that he were her brother so others would not misinterpret their demonstrations of love.[8] As they are about to leave the royal palace together, she tells the court ladies that she only wants her beloved. She needs him to support her weary body, which is exhausted after her final intense and emotional appearance before the king (*cf.* Sgs 2^6).

"3) Let his left hand be under my head
And his right hand support me" (Sgs 8:3 – CDG).

Because she is in a hurry to depart, she repeats a shortened rendering of the admonition she had previously given to the court ladies (*cf.* Sgs 2^7, 3^5):

"4) Daughters of Jerusalem, I charge you:
Do not arouse or awaken love until it so desires."
(Sgs 8:4 – NIV)

She admonishes the court ladies for the third and final time that they should not attempt to interfere with her love for her beloved shepherd.

This important warning is a vital reminder for all believers. The glamour this world has to offer will try to allure us, but it will soon fade away. Since we are espoused to our beloved Shepherd, we should not allow anyone or anything to turn our affections away from our devotion to Him.

Act 7 – Reunited With Her Beloved

Shulamite and her beloved shepherd reminisce where they first fell in love and their blessed story of love.
(Song of Songs 8:5 to 8:14)

Scene 1 (8^5 to 8^7)
(Shulamite with her beloved on their way home.)

The young maiden leaves the royal palace in Jerusalem and travels with her beloved shepherd the long journey towards their home over 50 miles to the north.

Companions of the Shepherd
"5) Who is this coming up from the wilderness
Leaning on her beloved?"
(Sgs 8:5[a] – NAS)

As the Shulamite and the young shepherd near their rustic village, some of the shepherd's friends notice their approach. This scene is in stark contrast to a short time earlier when the young maiden arrived in Jerusalem with the king (*cf.* Sgs 3:6-11). Then she was riding in Solomon's royal train as he dazzled her with his stately carriage furnished with a lavish couch. She was traveling with the king, who offered her all the finer things his great wealth could provide, but who wanted her for her beautiful body. Here she is seen walking, leaning on the one she dearly loves. While he is only a humble shepherd, he is her best friend who wants to spend the rest of his life caring for her.

This clearly speaks to the stark contrast between the choices every believer faces. We have given our hearts to our beloved Shepherd, but the world tries to lure our allegiance away by offering us seemingly attractive pleasures and trinkets of this life that will pass away. Like the Shulamite, our choice is clear.

Shulamite

"5) Under this apple-tree I won thy heart,
Here thy mother travailed, Here laboring she gave thee birth."
(Sgs 8:5^{b-d} – CDG)

As the young couple approach their village, they arrive at the place where they first fell in love, which was also under the tree where the young shepherd was born. It was here, under this lovely fruit tree, that they made their original commitment to one another. This sacred spot is where they exchanged their vows of faithfulness and love. As they remember that special time, the young maiden repeats her vow to her beloved:

"6) Oh, place me as a seal upon thy heart,
As a seal upon thine band!
For love is strong as death,
Affection as inexorable as Hades.
Its flames are flames of fire,
The flames of the Eternal."
(Sgs 8:6 – CDG)

The Shulamite had a deep love for her beloved shepherd that was sparked from the divine love of God. Because the young maiden allowed this very passion for her beloved shepherd to rule her heart, this divine love helped her endure. When put to the most severe test, it was able to withstand all the many trials and temptations by King Solomon and the court ladies, as they tried to lure her away from her beloved shepherd.

Similarly, as believers, we made our vows to our beloved Shepherd when we came to the old rugged cross (tree) at Calvary and made our commitment to Him. If we remain faithful to Him, by allowing God's divine love to rule our hearts, we can be more than conquerors in any situation because of the mighty power of His love (*cf.* Rom 8:37)[1]. By allowing His love to control our life, we can overcome all the many trials and temptations we face. His great love came to set the captives free (*cf.* Isa 61:1, Luk 4:18)[2], and because it is victorious over death, it is even stronger than death itself (1Co 15:54-55)[3].

Like death, genuine love will not let go of the person who is the object of that love. The devout affection the Shulamite had for her beloved emanated from the Almighty. Being divine love, it is more powerful than any power on earth.

> *"7) Floods cannot quench love; Streams cannot sweep it away.*
> *If one should offer all his wealth for love,*
> *He would be utterly despised"* (Sgs 8:7 – CDG).

As water is used to extinguish the flames of fire, this metaphor reveals that divine love cannot be influenced. Such love cannot be purchased, no matter what the price. While the king attempted to win the young maiden through his many flatteries and great wealth, it could not be bought. True love is priceless.

The great love between the young maiden and her beloved is a reflection of the love God has for His people. The prophet Isaiah tells how the Lord promises to provide secure protection:

> *"When you pass through the waters, I will be with you;*
> *And through the rivers, they shall not overflow you.*
> *When you walk through the fire, you shall not be burned,*
> *Nor shall the flame scorch you"* (Isa 43:2 – NKJV).

As noted by one commentator regarding the similarity "between 8:6-7 of the Canticle and Isa 43:2…The peace and security of the eschatological era is thus evoked…in [Isa 43:2], which affirms that nothing can again disturb the tranquil and profound attachment of the Bride returned to her Beloved" (Pope, p. 674).

God's love will always endure. The Shulamite's devotion and passionate love for her beloved is a reflection of that love.

Scene 2 ($8^8$to 8^{12})
(Shulamite and her beloved shepherd travel home.)

The young maiden and her beloved then travel to her home where she discusses with her brothers how great her temptations with the king really were. Because of her faithfulness in keeping herself a chaste young maiden, they agree to reward her.

Once the young couple arrive at the Shulamite's home, her brothers remind her how they had promised to reward her if she remained a virtuous woman for when she is married.

One of the Brothers of the Shulamite
"8) Our sister is still young,
And is not yet marriageable.
What shall we do for our sister,
When she shall be demanded in marriage?

Another Brother
9) If she be like a wall,
We will build upon her a silver turret.
But if she be like a door,
We will enclose her with boards of cedar."
(Sgs 8:8-9 – CDG)

The brothers were concerned for their only sister. They desired for her to be married when she was ready, but wanted her to be a woman of virtue – a pure virgin with high moral character. To induce her to become such a woman, they pledged to highly reward her by giving her a "*silver turret*," which was probably a "*silver horn*, a highly prized ornament which women wore on their heads" (Ginsburg, p. 189), "perhaps for her marriage, as the bride in ancient times wore a crown" (Harper, p. 60). If she remained like a wall, symbolizing a virtuous bride who resisted the advances and temptations that tried and tested her loyalty and faithfulness, she would be rewarded with a crown of silver for her wedding. But if she were a door, symbolizing she was promiscuous; they would restrict her with "*boards of cedar*." A wall represents an impregnable fortress able to withstand unwanted advances or attacks (*cf.* Sgs 4^{12}); while a door would easily allow her to be seduced, thereby losing her chastity.

Shulamite
"10) I am like a wall, And my bosom is as towers!
Then I was in his eyes
As one that findeth favour."
(Sgs 8:10 – CDG)

The young maiden tells her brothers that she is a wall – a virtuous maiden who resisted the enticements and inducements that tried and tested her commitment to her beloved. Since she was successful in remaining a chaste virgin, in her brothers' eyes she was due the reward they had promised her. She endured every trial and temptation to the end, and she earned the crown of silver for remaining a loyal and devoted bride.

In a similar manner, the believer's commitment toward our beloved Shepherd is put to the test as the world (typified by Solomon) attempts to draw us away from our devotion to Him. If we are able to succeed by following the young Shulamite's example, we will also be richly rewarded when we stand before the Judgement Seat of Christ (*cf.* 2Cr 5:10), where we can receive many different types of crowns[4] and rewards for remaining a devoted, pure (chaste) virgin for our Bridegroom.

"I am jealous for you with a godly jealousy.
I promised you to one husband, to Christ,
*so that I might **present you as a pure virgin to him.***
But I am afraid that just as Eve was deceived by the serpent's
*cunning, your minds **may somehow be led astray from your***
sincere and pure devotion to Christ" (2Cr 11:2-3 – NIV).

The young maiden then reveals to her brothers the magnitude of what King Solomon offered her if she would forget her commitment to her beloved shepherd and accept the great wealth he could provide.

Shulamite

"11) Solomon had a vineyard in Baal-hammon;
He let out the vineyard to tenants;
Each of whom yielded for the fruit of it
A thousand shekels of silver.
12) **I will keep my own vineyard:**
Be the thousands thine, 0 Solomon,
And the two hundreds to the keepers of its fruit!"
(Sgs 8:11-12 – CDG)

Besides the difficult and widely interpreted sections found in 6:10-13 of the Song, the above two verses have presented commentators with a broad spectrum of suggestions as to their true meaning (see Pope, pp. 688-693). Where Solomon's vineyard is located, who the tenants were, and what the thousand shekels of silver represent are highly debated, based upon the reviewer's method of interpretation.

From a literal perspective, the Shulamite is telling her brothers that Solomon offered her his highly valued vineyard, which produced a sizeable crop. It was leased out to farmers or share-croppers, and each one paid one thousand shekels of silver every year with two hundred shekels going to the farmers. Ginsburg calculates the annual income from each tenant would be about 130 pounds of silver.[5] At today's value of over $15 per ounce, the yearly value of the crop from every farmer would be more than $28,000 each. With such a sizeable annual income, the total value of the vineyard was considerable. In addition to all the flatteries of the king and the court ladies, along with Solomon's ranking the Shulamite above all his other queens and concubines, this valuable piece of property would have been a tremendous inducement to any young maiden. However, she tells her brothers that she told the king to keep his precious property and that she will keep her own vineyard (*cf.* Sgs 1:6) to share with her beloved shepherd. Her own vineyard is both her own land, as well as metaphorically, her own person, which she plans to share with her beloved.

Scene 3 (8^{13} and 8^{14})
(Shulamite and her beloved shepherd's closing words.)

The young maiden is so happy to be home that she goes out to her favorite spot, the garden, where she and her beloved shepherd would spend time together. Friends of the young shepherd come visit the joyful maiden where they witness the tender love and devotion she has for her beloved.

The Shepherd
"13) 0 thou that dwellest in the gardens,
My companions are listening to thy voice,
Let me hear thy voice!" (Sgs 8:13 – CDG)

The companions of the shepherd who observed the young couple's arrival earlier (Sgs 8^5) have arrived near the garden where the Shulamite is now residing. Her beloved shepherd then asks her to tell his friends her recent experience with the king and its final outcome. The young shepherd wants them to hear, from her own mouth, who has won her heart.

The young maiden's heart is filled with joy as she sits in her pleasant and secluded retreat, reflecting upon how much she loves her beloved shepherd.

Shulamite
"14) Haste, 0 my beloved,
And be like the gazelle, as the young one of the hind,
Over the mountains of spices."
(Sgs 8:14 – CDG)

The Shulamite calls upon her beloved to come as quickly as possible to take her with him to their awaiting home. She made a similar appeal earlier, as she was residing in the king's royal tent (*cf.* Sgs 2$^{16\&17}$), when she was apart from her beloved because of the mountains of separation. Now that she has been set free from Solomon's clutches, they are able to reside in their *"mountain of spices,"* where they can enjoy the delightful bliss of each other's companionship for the rest of their lives.

In this final scene of this magnificent Song of Songs, we can almost hear the voice of our beloved Shepherd crying out for His devoted bride, to tell all those who are listening, our fondest heart's desire. Like the Shulamite, we are eagerly longing to be with our dear Bridegroom who has gone away to prepare a place for us (*cf.* Jhn 14:2). We want Him to come quickly, and to take us away to be with Him in our mountain home, the New Jerusalem (*cf.* Rev 21:2, 10).

The young maiden's devotion and faithfulness to her beloved shepherd has ignited a flame in our hearts to passionately cry out, *"O Beloved, come quickly for us!"*

"Even so, come, Lord Jesus."
(Rev 22:20)

Epilogue

The Bible is God's love letter to all of mankind. It begins in a garden with a man and a woman whose responsibility was to watch over it (Gen 2:8, 15). Because of their disobedience, they were sent out from the paradise God had prepared for them (Gen 3:23-24). To remedy the separation between God and mankind, He sent his only Son to restore people back into the relationship that He initially intended.

Approximately halfway into His word, in the middle of the Bible, He placed a love song designed to reveal the way He meant for a man and a woman to love one another. In this beautiful story of love, the woman is the heroine, exhibiting true virtue and fidelity toward her beloved. By remaining faithful to her espoused, she teaches us God's design for all men and women toward each other, and in their relationship with Him.

The last book in the Bible reveals how men and women will return to paradise, as God had originally planned, to reside with Him in the restored new heaven and earth (Rev 21:1-7).

The Bridegroom has gone to prepare a place for anyone who desires to come and to freely enjoy the water of life that He will provide.

*"17) **And the Spirit and the bride say, 'Come!'***
And let him who hears say, 'Come!'
And let him who thirsts come.
Whoever desires, let him take the water of life freely."
(Rev 22:17 – NKJV)

While we eagerly await His soon return, may we all enjoy and apply the Shulamite's beautiful lessons on love to our daily lives. Let us join her by singing, *"Make haste, my beloved, and come quickly, like a gazelle or a young hart [and take me to our waiting home] upon the mountains of spices!"* (Sgs 8:14–AMP)

Even So Come
by Kristian Stanfill

All of creation

All of the earth

Make straight a highway

A path for the Lord

Jesus is coming soon

Call back the sinner

Wake up the saint

Let every nation

Shout of Your fame

Jesus is coming soon

Like a bride

Waiting for her groom

We'll be a church

Ready for You

Every heart longing for our King

We sing

Even so come

Lord Jesus come

© 2015 Kristian Stanfill. All Rights Reserved.

To view a recent YouTube video of this beautiful song, please see our article entitled *Even So Come* on the **Recent Posts** section on our website (www.ProphecyCountdown.com).

Reference Notes

Prologue to Introduction

1) Driver, S.R.– *An Introduction to the Literature of the Old Testament*, The World Publishing Company © 1965, p. 437.

2) Ginsburg, Christian D. – *The Song of Songs,* Wipf and Stock Publishers, June 2009, p. 124, "The subject...is decisive against Solomon's authorship. It is impossible that he should describe himself as having attempted to gain the espoused affections of a country maiden, and being defeated by her virtue....the author of the book never...would he announce his own production as *"the finest or most celebrated Song."*

3) Duguid, Iain M. – *The Song of Songs*, InterVarsity Press, USA © 2015, p. 73, "The book contains the best of all songs because it concerns the greatest subject matter of all, which is love (I Cor. 13:13). It is clear...that the greatest song about love is likely not merely to speak of human love, but also to celebrate and teach us something about divine love that God has for his people (Isa. 5:1-7)."

Act 1 – Love Between Two Lovers

1) Online Dictionary, © 2015 Dictionary.com, LLC. Soliloquy is defined as "an utterance or discourse by a person who is talking to himself or herself or is disregardful of or oblivious to any hearers present (often used as a device in drama to disclose a character's innermost thoughts): Hamlet's soliloquy begins with "To be or not to be." Also, a soliloquy is "a device often used in drama when a character speaks to himself or herself, relating thoughts and feelings, thereby also sharing them with the audience, giving off the illusion of being a series of unspoken reflections." Courtesy of Wikipedia®, the Wikimedia Foundation, Inc., a non-profit organization.
https://en.wikipedia.org/wiki/Soliloquy#cite_note-1
Understanding how soliloquies are used helps explain how the Shulamite's dialogue with her shepherd lover allows the audience to feel like her lover is present, even when he is not. (accessed 11/6/15).

Act 1 – Love Between Two Lovers (continued)

2) Ginsburg, op.cit. p. 136.

3) Verses cited regarding the good Shepherd:

> *"11) I am the **good shepherd**: the **good shepherd** giveth his life for the sheep.....14) I am the **good shepherd**, and know my sheep, and am known of mine"* (Jhn 10:10-11, 14).

> *"Now the God of peace, that brought again from the dead our Lord Jesus, that **great shepherd** of the sheep..."* (Heb 13:20)

> *"For you were like sheep going astray, but have now returned to the Shepherd and Overseer of your souls"* (1Pe 2:25 – NKJV).

4) For an interesting study of the lily and how it is used elsewhere in scripture, please see our article entitled: ***The Magnificent Lily*** that can be found under the **Recent Posts** section of our website: www.ProphecyCountdown.com

Act 2 – Longing During Separation

1) Carr, Rev G. Lloyd – ***The Song of Solomon: An Introduction & Commentary***, InterVarsity Press © 1984, p. 99.

2) While Jesus tells us that the generation will not pass away before all things are accomplished, we do not know for sure how long a generation may be. For this reason, Jesus told us to always watch and pray for that glorious day (Luk 21:34-36).

3) After the budding of the fig tree, which represents the nation of Israel being formed in 1948, the prophet Jeremiah mentions the judgement of Moab in chapter 48, followed by the judgement of Babylon in chapters 50 and 51. For a detailed look into the events prophesied to take place during the tribulation period, please see our recent commentary on the book of Revelation: ***Calling All Overcomers***, which can be freely downloaded from our website: www.ProphecyCountdown.com

4) Ginsburg, op.cit. p. 148. While some commentators suggest that the term *"shadows flee away"* refers to the sunrise, Ginsburg gives an excellent argument why this refers to the sunset, where "the shadows are said to flee away when at sunset they become elongated and stretched out; thus as it were run away from us, further and further, till they eventually vanish in the dark of night. Hence David speaking of the approaching sunset of his life, says, *My days are like an elongated shadow*, Ps. cii.12; cix 23."

Act 3 – Dream for Soulmate

1) Please see Appendix 4 in *Calling All Overcomers*, which provides a more in-depth analysis of the Olivet Discourse. In this important teaching Jesus gave right before His crucifixion, Matthew recorded three separate questions the disciples asked. Jesus' response essentially addressed three different groups of people. This division can be seen by making the following proper partition of Matthew's account:

Jews	Mat 24:4-31
Church	Mat 24:32 to Mat 25:30
Gentiles	Mat 25:31-46

Act 4 – Offer to Rescue

1) Harper, Rev. Andrew – *The Song of Solomon – With Introduction and Notes*, Kessinger Publishing, LLC © 2010, re-published from Cambridge University Press © 1902, p. 24.

2) Upon seeing his lovely bride-to-be for the first time (after a brief separation), the beloved shepherd tells her, *"You have captivated my heart with one glance of your eyes, with one jewel from your necklace"* (Sgs 4:9 – ESV). The passionate emotion the young shepherd must have experienced upon seeing the love of his life was partially captured in the famous, modern-day love scene in the 1996 film *Jerry Maguire*. Those familiar with the movie will recall Dorothy's well-known line, *"You had me at hello."* In this scene, actress Renée Zellweger vividly portrays the instantaneous fervor the young shepherd must have felt with just one look from his beloved. Dorothy's passion for her returning husband is mirrored in the shepherd's emboldened heart with just one glance from her eyes. To see a brief YouTube video clip of this memorable scene, please see the **Supplemental Articles** on our website under the tab for this book: www.ProphecyCountdown.com.

Act 5 – Dream of Separation

1) Clarence Larkin's depiction of the foolish virgins can be found on page 20 in his book, *The Second Coming of Christ*, as listed in the bibliography. This rendering shows the 5 foolish virgins sleeping and unprepared for the return of the bridegroom for the wedding. As a result, the door was shut and these foolish virgins were not allowed entrance. The door being shut to the lukewarm believers is an allusion to the coming separation among believers when the Lord returns. While the five wise virgins who are prepared are allowed to enter into the wedding, the foolish virgins were shut out causing them to endure a period of chastisement (Rev 3:19) for not being ready.

2) The Scriptures teach that the Lord chastens his own because He loves all believers as His own son:

> *"11) My son, despise not the chastening of the LORD; neither be weary of his correction: 12) For whom the LORD loveth he correcteth; even as a father the son in whom he delighteth"* (Pro 3:11-12).

> *"5) And ye have forgotten the exhortation which speaketh unto you as unto children, My son, despise not thou the chastening of the Lord, nor faint when thou art rebuked of him: 6) For whom the Lord loveth he chasteneth, and scourgeth every son whom he receiveth"* (Heb 12:5-6).

Act 6 – Longing for Her Lover

1) Bullinger, E. W., *Number in Scripture*, Kregel Publications © 1967, p. 243.

2) Taylor, J. Hudson – *Union and Communion: Thoughts on the Song of Solomon*, © 2012, p. 49.

3) The original Hebrew and Greek text place verse 13 as the first verse of the next chapter (i.e., 7^1). Most English versions place this verse as the last verse in the chapter (i.e., 6^{13}). The numbering of the English versions is followed in this writing.

4) Please see the article on the *The Separation* that can be found on the First Fruit website (accessed 1/26/2016):
http://www.ffruits.org/v03/theseparation.html

5) Most modern Bible translations incorrectly have the Shulamite speaking in verse 9, interrupting the king as he tells the young maiden how her mouth is like fine wine. Ginsburg, however, strongly objects by noting, "But it is incredible that this modest woman would approve of these expressions with regard to her own person..." (Ginsburg, p. 181). Pope goes on to state: "Ginsburg's reaction to the line indicates that he sensed a rather strong erotic suggestiveness: 'We earnestly request those who maintain the allegorical interpretation of the Song seriously to reflect whether this verse, and indeed the whole of this address, can be put into the mouth of Christ speaking to the Church. Would not our minds recoil with horror were we to hear a Christian using it publicly, or even privately, to illustrate the love of Christ for his Church?'" (Pope, p. 635).

6) The things offered by the world will quickly fade away.

> *"15) **Love not the world**, neither the **things that are in the world**. If any man love the world, the love of the Father is not in him. 16) For all that is in the world, the **lust of the flesh**, and the **lust of the eyes**, and the **pride of life**, is not of the Father, but is of the world. 17) **And the world passeth away**, and the **lust thereof:** but he that doeth the will of God abideth..."* (1Jo 2:15-17).

7) As the young maiden had already made the commitment to her beloved shepherd, so have we, as believers, given our hearts to our Beloved. Like Joshua we must choose who we will serve:

> *"But if serving the Lord seems undesirable to you, then choose for yourselves this day whom you will serve, whether the gods your ancestors served beyond the Euphrates, or the gods of the Amorites, in whose land you are living. **But as for me and my household, we will serve the Lord**"* (Jos 24:15 – NIV).

8) "What she desires is freedom to love him and to express that love. Had he been her brother she would have had that liberty. Only the brother and the father's brother's son have among the Bedouin the right to kiss a maiden" (Harper, p. 54).

Act 7 – Reunited With Her Beloved

1) As believers, we can be more than conquerors in any situation because of the mighty power of His love: *"35) Who shall separate us from the love of Christ? Shall tribulation, or distress, or persecution, or famine, or nakedness, or peril, or sword? 37) **Yet in all these things we are more than conquerors through Him who loved us.** 38) For I am persuaded that neither death nor life, nor angels nor principalities nor powers, nor things present nor things to come, 39) nor height nor depth, nor any other created thing, shall be able to separate us from the love of God which is in Christ Jesus our Lord"* (Rom 8:35, 37-39 – NKJV).

2) The prophet Isaiah prophesied things Christ would do and the Apostle Luke recorded the Lord's words in his first sermon:

> *"The Spirit of the Lord GOD is upon me; because the LORD hath anointed me to preach good tidings unto the meek; he hath sent me to bind up the brokenhearted, **to proclaim liberty to the captives**, and the opening of the prison to them that are bound;"* (Isa 61:1)

> *"The Spirit of the Lord is on Me, because He has anointed Me to preach good news to the poor. He has sent Me **to proclaim freedom to the captives** and recovery of sight to the blind, to set free the oppressed,"* (Luk 4:18 – HCSB)

3) The Apostle Paul taught the church at Corinth how Christ ultimately defeats Death, obtaining victory over the grave:

> *"54) So when this corruptible shall have put on incorruption, and this mortal shall have put on immortality, then shall be brought to pass the saying that is written, Death is swallowed up in victory. 55) O death, where is thy sting? O grave, where is thy victory?"* (1Co 15:54-55)

4) For a detailed look at the Judgement Seat of Christ, and the various crowns that can be obtained for our faithfulness, please see pp. 15-23 in *The Kingdom* that can be freely downloaded from our website: www.ProphecyCountdown.com

5) Ginsburg calculates the value of the vineyard he offered to give to the young maiden, as follows: "The shekel of the sanctuary, however, like all the weights and measures of the Temple, was computed at double the ordinary. See Ezek.xlv.12, 1 Kings x. 17, comp. with 2 Chron. ix. 16,...A thousand shekels, therefore would be about one hundred and thirty pounds. Remembering that each of the farmers had to pay this sum annually, and that money in those days had according to Michaelis...fifty times its present value, we shall be able to judge of the allurement which this ample estate offered" (Ginsburg, p. 190).

Appendix 2 – Three Character Storyline

1) Pope, Marvin H. – *Song of Songs A New Translation with Introduction and Commentary*, Doubleday © 1977, p. 198, While Ewald was a forerunner in developing the three character storyline view, certain elements of his interpretation are considered questionable by some expositors. This becomes particularly evident when reading the detailed exegeses made in Christian D. Ginsburg's fine commentary, which is listed in the bibliography.

Appendix 3 – Psalm 45: A Royal Wedding

1) See pp. 57-61 in *Calling All Overcomers* to see why we believe Christ is the rider on the white horse under the 1st Seal.

2) See pp. 36-37 in *Calling All Overcomers* for further details describing the two garments of the believer.

3) In order to fully understand the two garments of the believer it is important to remember that the believers' righteousness provided by Christ is completely obtained by faith.

> "Even the righteousness of God which is by faith of Jesus Christ unto all and upon all them that believe" (Rom 3:22).

The believer receives the righteousness of God by faith in Jesus Christ + nothing! Eminent Professor Beal's perceptive exegesis of Rev 19:7-8, which follows, brings to light the believers' responsibility in preparing for their marriage:

Appendix 3 – Psalm 45: A Royal Wedding (continued)
Beal, G.K. – *Revelation: A Shorter Commentary*, William B.
Eerdmans Publishing Company © 2015, pp. 403-406:
"The bride is said to have prepared herself for the marriage,
which places the emphasis on the bride's responsibility in
making herself ready...[its] better to view vv. 7-8 as suggesting
that a transformed life is not only the proper response but in fact
a *necessary* response. White clothes in Revelation, when worn
by the saints, always signify *a gift from God given* to those with
tested and purified faith...the white clothes are not merely the
saints' righteous acts but the *reward for* or *result of* such acts...
The final clause of v. 8 could thus be paraphrased: "the fine
linen is the reward for or result of the saints' righteous deeds."

"The OT background to the passage is Isa. 61:10, where the
Lord clothes His people with "garments of salvation" and "a
robe of righteousness...And as a bride adorns herself..." Isaiah's
phrases underscore the activity of God in providing these
clothes. This righteousness comes ultimately from God...
though the concept of the necessary response of righteous acts
by the saints is vital...This underscores the aspect of human
accountability highlighted by v.7b: "His bride has made herself
ready." Yet...God has provided grace for them to cloth
themselves now by the power of the Spirit."

4) See pp. 152-156 in *Calling All Overcomers* for a look at
how the Apostle John describes the magnificent New Jerusalem.

5) Many believe Psa 45:9-15 describes Solomon as the king
with his many wives and concubines, which represent the
daughters of Gentile kings (*cf.* 1Ki 11:1,3). Here we see
Solomon in a positive sense, to typify Christ as the King with
his Church, which is comprised of Gentile believers from every
tribe and tongue and people and nation (Rev 5:9).

Appendix 5 – The Bride of Christ

1) Some of the material included in Appendix 5 was adopted
from a tract written by Pastor John Lanham (deceased) who
founded the Chattanooga Bible Institute.

Bibliography

Commentaries on the Song of Songs
The key to the approaches used in the following commentaries:
L-Literal, A-Allegorical, T-Typological, E-Eclectic, P-Prophecy

Burrowes, Rev. George – *A Commentary on the Song of Solomon*, William S. Martien © 1853, Republished by Forgotten Books © 2012 [A]*

Carr, Rev. G. Lloyd – *The Song of Solomon: An Introduction and Commentary*, InterVarsity Press © 1984 [L]*

Dillow, Joseph C. – *Solomon On Sex: A Biblical Guide to Married Love*, Thomas Nelson Publishers © 1977 [L]

Duguid, Iain M. – *The Song of Songs: An Introduction and Commentary*, InterVarsity Press, © 2015 [E]**

Durham, James – *The Song of Solomon*, Work originally published in 1864, Republished by Klock & Klock Christian Publishers © 1981 [A]

Driver, S. A. – *An Introduction to the Literature of the Old Testament: Song of Songs*, Meridian Books. ©1897 [E]**

Fausset, A. R. – *A Commentary on the Song of Solomon:* An Introduction to the Poetical Books, Originally published in 1871, Courtesy www.BlueLetterBible.org, [A]

Gill, John – *An Exposition of the Book of Solomon's Song Commonly Called Canticles*, Originally published in 1724, Republished by Forgotten Books, © 2015 [A]

Ginsburg, Christian D. – *The Song of Songs: Translated from the Original Hebrew with a Commentary, Historical and Critical*, Wipf and Stock Publishers, June 2009, Work originally published in May 1857 [L]***

Glickman, Dr. Craig – *Solomon's Song of Love*, Howard Publishing Co. © 2004 [L]*

Harper, Rev. Andrew – *The Song of Solomon – With Introduction and Notes*, Kessinger Publishing, LLC © 2010, Work originally published by Cambridge: at the University Press © 1902 [L]**

Commentaries on the Song of Songs (continued)
The key to the approaches used in the following commentaries:
L-Literal, A-Allegorical, T-Typological, E-Eclectic, P-Prophecy

Henry, Matthew – *Commentary on the Whole Bible: An Exposition, With Practical Observations of the Song of Solomon*, Fleming H. Revell Company, Work originally published in 1710 [T]*

Lee, Witness – *Holy Bible Recovery Version*, Living Stream Ministry © 2003 [T]

McPhee, L. M. – *The Romance of the Ages*, Designed Products, Inc. © 1950 [T]*

Nee, Watchman – *Song of Songs: Unveiling the Mystery of Intimacy with Christ*, CLC Publications © 1965 [T]

Parnell, Diane – *Discovering God's Heart: A Journey Through the Song of Solomon*, www.equipper.com [T]

Pope, Marvin H. – *Song of Songs A New Translation with Introduction and Commentary*, Doubleday © 1977 [L]*

Provan, Iain – *The NIV Application Commentary Series: Ecclesiastes, Song of Songs*, Zondervan © 2001 [E]

Rudd, Steve – *Lovesick: A Commentary on the Song of Solomon, Canticles: God's Marriage Preparation Manual*, Steve Rudd © 2013 www.bible.ca [T]*

Simmons, Brian – *Song of Songs: The Journey of the Bride*, Insight Publishing Group © 2002 [A]

Tanner, J. Paul – *The Message of the Song of Songs*, Bibliotheca Sacra 154 article (June 1997):142-61 [L]*

Taylor, J. Hudson – *Union and Communion: Thoughts on the Song of Solomon*, © 2012 [T]

Unger, Merrill F. – *Unger's Bible Handbook: Son of Solomon Sanctity of Wedded Love*, Moody Press © 1966 [T]

Wesley, John – *Song of Solomon: Explanatory Notes and Commentary*, Work originally published in 1765 [A]

Young, Edward J. – *An Introduction to the Old Testament: Song of Solomon*, W.B. Eerdmans Pub. Co. © 1989 [E]
* Most useful commentaries in this author's opinion.

Other Works Consulted

Beal, G.K. – *Revelation: A Shorter Commentary*, William B. Eerdmans Publishing Company © 2015

Bullinger, E. W., *Number in Scripture Its Supernatural Design and Spiritual Significance*, Kregel Publications © 1967

Chambers, Oswald – *The Oswald Chambers Devotional Bible*, English Standard Version, Crossway © 2009

Church, J.R. – *Hidden Prophecies In The Psalms*, Prophecy Publications © 1986

Dahl, Mikkel – *Repent! What Does That Mean?*, Shepherds-field Publishers © 2000

Gallagher, Steve – *The Time of Your Life In Light of Eternity*, Pure Life Ministries © 2006, www.EternalWeight.com

Ironside, Harry A. – *Except Ye Repent*, Baker Book House, Originally printed in 1937, the American Tract Society

Larkin, Rev. Clarence – *The Second Coming of Christ*, Rev. Clarence Larkin Estate © 1918-1922. Pictures shown in this book are used with permission of the Rev. Clarence Larkin Estate, P.O. Box 334 Glenside, PA 19038, USA, 215-576-5590, www.larkinestate.com

Mize, Lyn – Article from First Fruit Ministries website: *The Separation*, Available at: www.ffruits.org

Panton, D. M. – *The Judgment Seat of Christ*, Schoettle Publishing Co. Inc., © 1984, www.schoettlepublishing.com

Shupe, Pastor Randy – *The Glory of His Inheritance: The Bride of Christ*, © 1986, www.PastorRandyShupe.com

Strong, James H. – *Strong's Exhaustive Concordance*, Baker Books © 1992

Vine, W.E. – *Vine's Complete Expository Dictionary Of Old And New Testament Words*, Thomas Nelson © 1996

Watson, George D. – *Bridehood Saints*, Harvey and Tait Publishers © 1988

Zajac, John – *The Delicate Balance*, Prescott Press, Inc. and Huntington House, Inc. @1989

ABBREVIATIONS

Books of the Bible

Old Testament (OT)

Genesis (Gen)
Exodus (Exd)
Leviticus (Lev)
Numbers (Num)
Deuteronomy (Deu)
Joshua (Jos)
Judges (Jdg)
Ruth (Rth)
1 Samuel (1Sa)
2 Samuel (2Sa)
1 Kings (1Ki)
2 Kings (2Ki)
1 Chronicles (1Ch)
2 Chronicles (2Ch)
Ezra (Ezr)
Nehemiah (Neh)
Esther (Est)
Job (Job)
Psalms (Psa)
Proverbs (Pro)

Ecclesiastes (Ecc)
Solomon (Sgs)
Isaiah (Isa)
Jeremiah (Jer)
Lamentations (Lam)
Ezekiel (Eze)
Daniel (Dan)
Hosea (Hsa)
Joel (Joe)
Amos (Amo)
Obadiah (Oba)
Jonah (Jon)
Micah (Mic)
Nahum (Nah)
Habakkuk (Hab)
Zephaniah (Zep)
Haggai (Hag)
Zechariah (Zec)
Malachi (Mal)

New Testament (NT)

Matthew (Mat)
Mark (Mar)
Luke (Luk)
John (Jhn)
Acts (Act)
Romans (Rom)
1 Corinthians (1Cr)
2 Corinthians (2Cr)
Galatians (Gal)
Ephesians (Eph)
Philippians (Phl)
Colossians (Col)
1 Thessalonians (1Th)
2 Thessalonians (2Th)

1 Timothy (1Ti)
2 Timothy (2Ti)
Titus (Tts)
Philemon (Phm)
Hebrews (Hbr)
James (Jam)
1 Peter (1Pe)
2 Peter (2Pe)
1 John (1Jo)
2 John (2Jo)
3 John (3Jo)
Jude (Jud)
Revelation (Rev)

Appendix 1 – Approaches to the Song of Songs

Literal (Natural)	Allegorical (Spiritual) (Jews & Christians)	Typological (Figurative) (OT as Type)	Prophetic	Eclectic Blending of Views
Lloyd Carr	Origen	Unger	Johannes Cocceius (1699)	Iain Duguid
Pope	Augustine	Matthew Henry	John Cotton (1648)	Iain Provan***
Dr. Glickman	Wesley	Delitzsch	Hennischius (1688)	Harman***
Dillow	Burrowes	Hudson Taylor		
J.T. Jacobi***(1771)	James Durham	Witness Lee		
H. Ewald***(1826)	John Gill(1724)	Watchman Nee		
Ginsburg***(1857)	Ibn Ezra***(1153)	L.M. McPhee		
S.R. Driver***(1897)				
Harper***(1902)				
Regained popularity last 200 years	Dominate view since Augustine			

*** Believe the Song centers around 3 people: Solomon, Shulamite maiden & shepherd lover.

The chart on the previous page summarizes the five major approaches to interpreting the Song of Songs.

Literal (Natural)

One of the oldest methods of interpreting the Song was to view it for what it appears to represent naturally: a series of love poems describing the affections two lovers share between one another. In the natural view it shows the mutual love and intimacy of two young people with explicit details of all of their desires and feelings toward one another along with all of their hopes, fears and concerns for that relationship. This approach came under attack by some of the early Church fathers, such as Origen, Augustine, and Jerome. They condemned the literal view in favor of their allegorical method of interpretation and they felt the literal reading should be eliminated.

Origen sought to "transform it into a spiritual drama free from all carnality. The reader was admonished to mortify the flesh and to take nothing predicated of the Song with reference to bodily functions, but to apply everything toward apprehension of the divine senses of the inner man"(Pope, p. 115).

Allegorical (Spiritual) – Jews and Christians

In 550 AD, the Council of Constantinople banned the literal reading of the Song of Songs in favor of the allegorical method. The allegorical view has dominated both Jewish and Christian interpretations because it depicts the love of God for his people. For the Jewish readers it represents an allegory of the love of God for the nation of Israel, while Christians see the love of Christ for His Church.

Under the allegorical methods, the literal situation described in the text is ignored in favor of describing the deeper spiritual meaning the Scripture was meant to convey. While a metaphor is a figure of speech used to compare unrelated elements, an allegory is really an extended metaphor, describing things on a deeper note or in greater detail. The allegorical view attempts to bring out the deeper spiritual meaning of the text, by going beneath the surface, to uncover particular higher truths and principles that the literal reading describes. While the literal view focuses on the physical and emotional aspects of human love, the allegorical method of interpretation concentrates primarily on the spiritual facets of man's life.

Typological (Figurative) – Old Testament (OT) as Type
Somewhat similar to the allegorical view is the typological method of interpretation. While the allegorical view denies or ignores historical facts found in the OT account, the typological recognizes the OT accounts as types, which are forerunners that foreshadow events or teachings found in the New Testament. Remember that Jesus taught all things which were written about him in the OT must be fulfilled. The typological method applies aspects found in the text as types, figures, or patterns, which find their ultimate fulfillment elsewhere in the Scriptures. While the typological interpretation accepts the literal meaning, it then attempts to reveal how it is accomplished.

This typological technique of interpretation has also been known as the figurative method. Many teachings in Scripture can be viewed three different ways: literally, figuratively, and prophetically. The figurative approach seeks to find the pattern or prototype, which foreshadows things found elsewhere. For example, Adam was a symbol or a representation of Christ who was yet to come (Rom 5:14). The typological or figurative manner of interpretation seeks to explain the text by showing its ultimate fulfillment.

Prophetic
Over the centuries there have been a few interpretations by men who see prophetic applications in the Song of Songs. Cocceius, Cotton, Hennischius, as well as others, saw in the Song various prophecies to be fulfilled during Church history down to the end

of the age and the final judgment. Cocceius regarded the book as a prophetical narrative of the transactions and events that are to happen in the Church. Cotton and Hennischius held similar prophetical views. As discussed in the narrative in this book, the Song does have a prophetic application; particularly to those living during the last days of the Church age.

Eclectic

The above approaches to interpreting the Song of Songs have been the major methods utilized to help readers understand its meaning. Recently, many Bible scholars and teachers have developed what we would label an Eclectic view, which represents the blending of two or more of the approaches.

For example, Ian Duguid blends what he labels the spiritual approach and the natural approach. He sees the 'spiritual' encompassing all of the allegorical and typological interpretations stating: "...what binds them together is the common conviction that the primary meaning of the text is in terms of the spiritual relationship between God and his people..." while the natural approach associates its primary significance describing "human relationships" (Duguid, p. 28). In a similar manner, Ian Provan blends the literal (natural) with what he labels as parabolic, which he describes as a "broadly based 'allegorical' approach" (Provan, p. 254).

The Eclectic approach to the Song of Songs allows one to draw from the suitable aspects of each of the other methods of interpretation in order to provide the reader with a clearer picture of the meaning of the book. While no one view may be entirely correct, the blending of the various methods allows one to better understand God's message in the Song.

As stated earlier, we believe many teachings in Scripture can be viewed literally, figuratively, and prophetically. This author has therefore adopted the Eclectic approach in this book.

Appendix 2 – Three Character Storyline

The traditional interpretation of Solomon's famous song revolves around the king's love for a Shulamite maiden and her love for him. This two character storyline is the predominate view taken by most expositors; unfortunately this point of view has cloaked its true meaning.

During the 12th century, a Jewish Rabbi named Abraham Ibn Ezra gave an allegorical interpretation of the Song, which also included a literal view that, "the lovers are a shepherd and a shepherdess, and that the king is a separate and distinct person from the beloved shepherd" (Ginsburg, p. 46).

This important clue to the Song's real meaning led several other modern-day authors to further develop this important perspective. In the 18th century, J. T. Jacobi held that its purpose was to celebrate fidelity between a humble maiden who was engaged to a shepherd. King Solomon's attempt to allure her from her true love was unsuccessful and she remained faithful. And in the 19th century, the celebrated German scholar H. Ewald said the true meaning of this book, "celebrates chaste, virtuous, and sincere love, which no splendor is able to dazzle, nor flattery to seduce" (Ginsburg, p. 93).

A brief synopsis of Ewald's three character perspective follows:

"The story describes the trials of a beautiful maiden from Shunem or Shulem who was a shepherdess. She was in love with a shepherd of the village, but her brothers did not approve and they transferred her to work in the vineyards in the hope of keeping her away from her lover. One day she was seen by Solomon's servants as the king was en route to his summer resort in Lebanon.....Solomon who falls in love with her at first sight, sings of her beauty, and tries to induce her to abandon her shepherd and accept the love and luxury he offers. The court ladies also try to persuade her, but her heart belongs to her shepherd. She yearns for her true love and is taunted by the court ladies that he has rejected her. She speaks with her love......and dreams that he has come to rescue her....She awakes and rushes into the street to seek him, but she is maltreated [in her dream] by the watchmen who take her as a woman of the street. The king, finally convinced of the constancy of her love for the shepherd, allows her to return home. She is joined by her true lover and leaning on his arm, returns to her village. They pass the scenes so dear to them while she recounts her recent misfortunes. The story ends on a note of triumph. Her love could not be overcome by the lures of luxury. She assures her brothers that their concerns for her virtue were unwarranted. She has proved that love can endure."[1]

Ewald's storyline should help the reader better understand the main plot of the Song, which is difficult to comprehend when a person reads the narrative for the first time. Because the identity of the various speakers is not always given, the true meaning can easily be missed. This is further complicated by the fact that many different Bible translators actually change the entire plot by making a flawed judgment as to the correct speaker. Understanding the true storyline will assist the reader in perceiving the story, which at first glance, has little or no sensible sequence.

Following Ewald's exposition of this most beautiful Song, Christian D. Ginsburg produced a masterful, verse-by-verse exegesis, which further elucidates the wonderful message God has for His people. To help better understand the storyline, the following represents a brief summary from his lengthy introduction with certain sections *paraphrased* for clarity:

"The particular design of this book has been much disputed. It is here maintained, that, upon careful examination, it will be found to record an example of virtue in a young woman who encountered and conquered the greatest temptations, and was, eventually, rewarded; the simple narrative...is as follows. There was a family living at Shulem, consisting of a widowed mother, several sons, and one daughter, who maintained themselves by farming and pasturage....*Her bothers watched over her by teaching her* that prudence and virtue would be rewarded. <u>In the course of time...she met with a graceful shepherd youth, to whom she afterwards became espoused</u> [engaged]...One morning in the spring, (2^{8-14}) this youth invited her to accompany him into the field; but the brothers, overhearing the invitation, and anxious for the reputation of their sister...sent her to take care of the vineyards (2^{15}). The damsel, however, consoled her beloved and herself with the assurance that, though separated bodily, indissoluble ties subsisted between them, over which her brothers had no control (2^{16})....The evening now was the only time in which they could enjoy each other's company, as during the day, the damsel was occupied in the vineyards (2^{17}). On one occasion, when entering a garden, she accidentally came in the presence of King Solomon, who happened to be on a summer visit to her neighbourhood (6^{11-12}). Struck with the beauty of the damsel, the King conducted her to his royal tent, and there, assisted by his court-ladies, endeavoured with alluring flatteries and promises, to gain her affections; but without effect (1^{9-11}). Released from the King's presence, the damsel soon sought an interview with her beloved shepherd [even in her dreams $(3^{1-5)}$].

The King, however, took her with him to his capital in great pomp, in the hope of dazzling her with his splendor (3^{6-11}); but neither did this prevail: for while even there, she told her beloved shepherd, who had followed her into the capitol, and obtained a *meeting* with her (4^{1-16}), that she was anxious to *leave* the gaudy scene for her home. The shepherd, on hearing this, praised her constancy, and such a manifestation of their mutual attachment took place, that several of the court-ladies were greatly affected by it (5^{1e}).

The King, still determined, if possible to win her affections, watched for another favorable opportunity, and with flatteries and allurements, surpassing all that had been used before, tried to obtain his purpose [of alluring her to stay]. He promised to elevate her to the highest rank, and to raise her above all his concubines and queens, if she would comply with his wishes; but, faithful to her espousals [engagement], she refused all his overtures, *because* her affections were pledged to another. The King, convinced at last that he could not possibly prevail, was obliged to *let her go; and she and her beloved shepherd, returned to her home.* On their way home, they visited the tree under which they had first met, and there renewed their vows of fidelity to each other. On her arrival in safety at her home, her brothers, according to their promise, rewarded her greatly for her virtuous conduct" (Ginsburg, pp. 4-6).

Ginsburg skillfully summarized the Song's storyline by stating: "the Song of Songs teaches a great moral lesson, worthy of Divine inspiration….The Shulamite, espoused to her shepherd, is tempted by a mighty potentate [royal leader] with riches and pleasures to *win* her affections; but strengthened by the power of divine love, she resists all temptation, remains faithful to her beloved, and is ultimately rewarded. The people of God, espoused to 'the Shepherd and Bishop of their souls,' are tempted by the prince of this world to forsake their Lord, but, strengthened by grace divine, they resist all allurements, and eventually receive the crown of glory" (Ginsburg, p. vii).

Christian D. Ginsburg's commentary on the Song of Songs is one of the most thorough exegeses of this remarkable section of the Bible. Published in May 1857, this extraordinary masterpiece examines the history and origins of the text and provides a critical explanation in great detail. A PDF copy of this great work may be found under the **Supplemental Articles** for this book on our website: www.ProphecyCountdown.com

Appendix 3 – Psalm 45: A Royal Wedding

One of the most beautiful pictures of the marriage of the bride of Christ is found in Psalm 45. While many Bible students see an allusion to Christ in verse 6, where He is referred to in the New Testament (*cf.* Psa 45:6 and Heb 1:8), most believe it's the Psalms' only New Testament reference to the Messiah. Upon further analysis, the entire psalm can be seen as a representation of Christ coming to gather His bride from among the Gentiles.

As we pointed out in our commentary on the book of Revelation, *Calling All Overcomers*, we believe Christ is the rider on the white horse under the first seal (Rev 6:1-2). This is seen in Psalm 45:4-6, that shows Christ riding out conquering men's hearts with righteousness – precisely what the rider on John's white horse is doing. The bow that He is carrying represents the Word of God (*cf.* Hab 3:8-9), which is able to conquer men's hearts – one of the rider's main objectives.[1]

Christ is also alluded to as the King seeking His bride in verses 10 and 11 of the psalm as established in Deuteronomy 21:10-13. Here the warrior was allowed to take a beautiful woman who was captured from among the Gentiles and take her as his wife. Psalm 45 shows this as a type of Christ, with the King taking His bride, who is to forget her old life, and where she came from, and to make Him her Lord:

> *"Listen, O daughter, Consider and incline your ear;*
> *Forget your own people also, and your father's house;*
> *So the King will greatly desire your beauty; Because He*
> *is your Lord, worship Him"* (Psa 45:10-11 – NKJV).

So we see Psalm 45 picturing Jesus riding out, conquering a people from among the Gentiles seeking those who are willing to leave their old life behind to make Him the King of their heart and life. Those devoted to the King will become His bride to be clothed in beautiful garments.

> *"13) The royal daughter is all glorious within the palace; Her **clothing is woven with gold**. 14) She shall be brought to the King in **robes of many colors**; The virgins, her companions who follow her, shall be brought to You. 15) With gladness and rejoicing they shall be brought; They shall enter the King's palace."* (Psa 45:13-15 – NKJV)

Notice that the *"royal daughter,"* i.e. the bride, is clothed with two garments. The first one is clothing woven with gold, which alludes to the *"robe of righteousness"* that is the imputed righteousness provided by Christ (Isa 61:10)[2]. The second garment is described by the psalmist as *"robes of many colors."* This is a picture of the *"fine linen"* the bride of Christ is seen wearing:

> *"And to her it was granted to be arrayed in fine linen, clean and bright, for the fine linen is the righteous acts of the saints"* (Rev 19:8 – NKJV).

While all true Christians receive Christ's imputed righteousness when they are saved, the prudent and dedicated believers make certain that they also have their wedding dress prepared. The righteous acts or deeds of the saints are the things that set the bride of Christ apart. While she already has obtained her *"robe of righteousness"* by faith, she makes herself ready for the wedding by obtaining her *"fine linen,"* which represents her righteous life that she leads (conduct, acts, and deeds)[3]. The *"robes of many colors"* is a picture of the beautiful life that she leads because of her devotion to her King.

Finally, the royal daughter (bride), along with her companions (the rest of the Church), will enter into the King's palace, which represents the New Jerusalem described in the book of Revelation.[4] The Amplified version of these verses helps to bring out the important sections within the palace:

> *"13) The King's daughter in the inner part [of the palace] is all glorious...14) She shall be brought to the King in raiment of needlework; with the virgins, her companions that follow her...15) With gladness and rejoicing will they be brought; they will enter into the King's palace"* (Psa 45:13-15 – AMP).

The inner part of the palace is the place the King's daughter is brought where she experiences an intimate relationship with the King. Her companions then follow into the palace where they will all enjoy great gladness and rejoicing together. This is a perfect picture of the New Jerusalem where all of the redeemed will dwell with God for eternity.

While Psalm 45 may have been written to describe the royal wedding of an earthly King,[5] we can clearly see that this is also a Messianic Psalm describing the magnificent wedding of the bride of Christ to her Royal Bridegroom.

Remember, Jesus told the disciples on the road to Emmaus that all things written about Him in the Psalms would be fulfilled.

> *"Then He said to them, "These are the words which I spoke to you while I was still with you, that all things must be fulfilled which were written in the Law of Moses and the Prophets and **the Psalms** concerning Me."*
> (Luke 24:44 – NKJV)

Psalm 45 tells the amazing story of how Christ came to find a beautiful woman to become His royal bride. For almost 2,000 years He has been seeking those willing to leave their old life behind to become His glorious bride.

In a related way, the Song of Solomon tells the beautiful story of how a Shulamite maiden falls in love with a shepherd boy and is subsequently enticed by King Solomon to leave him for all the worldly riches and pleasures he can offer her.

However the Shulamite maiden forsakes the life the king can offer her because her heart belongs to her shepherd lover and her only desire is to be his devoted bride.

The following diagrams help summarize these great truths that are woven throughout God's marvelous word:

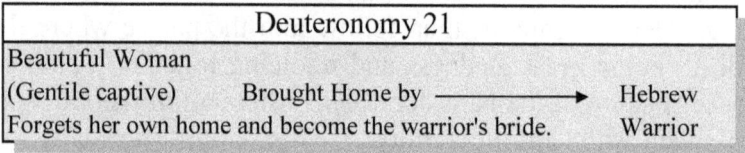

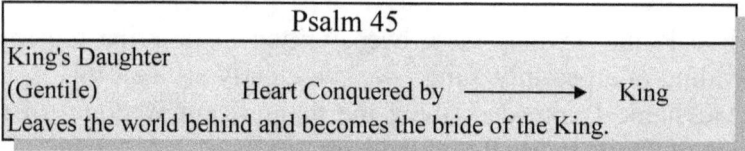

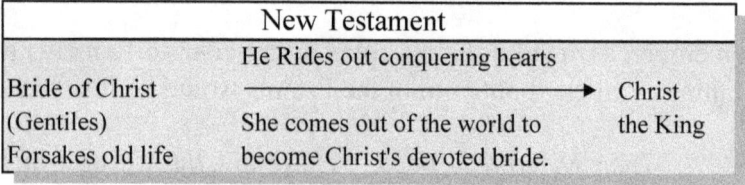

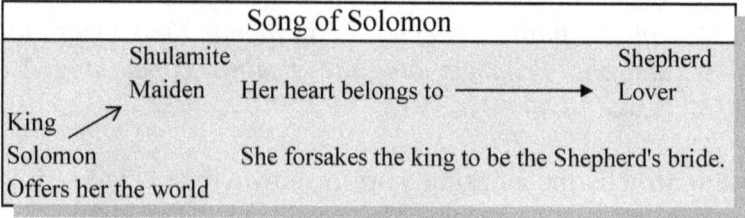

Deuteronomy 21

Beautiful Woman
(Gentile captive)   Brought Home by ⟶   Hebrew
Forgets her own home and become the warrior's bride.   Warrior

---

Psalm 45

King's Daughter
(Gentile)   Heart Conquered by ⟶   King
Leaves the world behind and becomes the bride of the King.

New Testament

                    He Rides out conquering hearts
Bride of Christ   ⟶   Christ
(Gentiles)   She comes out of the world to   the King
Forsakes old life   become Christ's devoted bride.

Song of Solomon

          Shulamite   Shepherd
          Maiden   Her heart belongs to ⟶   Lover
King ↗
Solomon   She forsakes the king to be the Shepherd's bride.
Offers her the world

Appendix 4 – The Ten Virgins

As alluded to in this beautiful Song, the Great God of Heaven has announced in His Holy Word that a grand wedding is about to take place. Mankind's time on this earth is about up, and the Bridegroom is getting ready to return for His bride. Are you part of the bride of Christ? Will you be ready when Jesus returns?

Who is it that is invited to the wedding banquet? It is those described in Rev 19:7 and 9:

> *"...For the wedding of the Lamb has come, and his bride has made herself ready...Then the angel said to me, "Write: Blessed are those who are invited to the wedding supper of the Lamb!" And he added "These are the true words of God"* (Rev 19:7,9 – NIV).

Notice that the above verse says, *"The bride made herself ready..."* How did she make herself ready?

> *"She was given fine linen to wear, bright and pure. For the fine linen represents the righteous acts of the saints"* (Rev 19:8 – HCSB).

The bride made herself ready for the wedding by obtaining her fine linen. This was her reward for her righteous life that she lived. The original Greek confirms that this fine linen is not the righteousness that is imputed to every believer in Christ, but represents the righteous acts or the righteous living of the believer (conduct, acts, and deeds) following their salvation. This same teaching was confirmed for us by Jesus when He taught about the ten virgins:

> *"1) Then the kingdom of heaven shall be likened to ten virgins who took their lamps and went out to meet the bridegroom. 2) Now five of them were wise, and five of them were foolish. Those who were foolish took their*

lamps and took no oil with them, 4) but the wise took oil in their vessels with their lamps. 5) But while the bridegroom was delayed, they all slumbered and slept. 6) And at midnight a cry was heard: 'Behold, the bridegroom is coming; go out to meet him!' 7) Then all those virgins arose and trimmed their lamps. 8) And the foolish said to the wise, 'Give us some of your oil, for our lamps are going out.' 9) But the wise answered, saying, 'No, lest there should not be enough for us and you; but go rather to those who sell, and buy for yourselves.' 10) And while they went to buy, the bridegroom came, and those who were ready went in with him to the wedding; and the door was shut."
(Mat 25:1-10 – NKJV)

Here we see that only the five wise virgins who were ready went to be with their Bridegroom. All 10 virgins were Christians because all did possess their oil, which represents the Holy Spirit who was given to each of them upon their conversion. The 5 foolish virgins, however, did not carry along the extra measure of oil that the 5 wise virgins carried in their jars. The 5 wise virgins were ready because they were obedient to the Word of God, which commands us to be *"filled with the Spirit"* (Eph 5:18). Because the 5 wise virgins were filled with the Spirit, they allowed Him to direct and empower their life.

It is important to note that the extra oil had to be bought by the foolish virgins (v.9). While the indwelling spirit is a free gift from God that cannot be bought, being filled by the Holy Spirit involves effort on the part of the Christian, requiring our submission to Him (Gal 5:16-25) in order to crucify the flesh and allow Him complete control. As a result, the 5 wise virgins were properly equipped when the Bridegroom arrived. The wise virgins were ready because of their faithfulness, while the foolish virgins were not prepared due to their own lethargy in providing their extra measure of oil to keep their lamps burning.

Are you a wise or foolish virgin today? If you are not sure, please consider making the following prayer right now:

> *"Dear God in Heaven, I realize that I have not really been living my life for you. I humbly turn to you right now and ask you to forgive me. Dear Jesus, please rule and reign in my heart and life. Please help me to live for you for whatever time remains. I pray that I may be ready and that I may be able to stand before you when you return for me. In Jesus' name I pray. Amen"*

Our prayer is that many in the Church will pray this prayer and ask the Lord to help them be prepared for His return. We do not know for certain when Jesus will return so we need to be ready every single day as we eagerly await His coming for us.

THE WISE VIRGINS
"They That Were Ready Went in with Him to the Marriage and the Door Was Shut."
Matt. 25:10.

A poem about the virgins in Matthew 25:1-13
THE BRIDE
A lamp with oil
All 10 did possess
But, remember, 5 were wise
And 5 were foolish.
Those who were wise
Heeded the call
By hearing God's voice:
"Give me your all"
The foolish however
Squandered their worth
They did not shine for Jesus
Nor the people on earth.
They heard "The Cry"
Along with the wise
This is how the foolish
Were taken by surprise:
Their light became impoverished
For their joy did not spread
The 'oil of gladness' for them
Flickered out instead.
But the wise grew brighter
With a special over-flow
The more they loved Jesus
They gained a purer glow.
Though the cry was mighty
Five questioned the call
They could not comprehend:
'Come give me your all.'
For if they truly loved Him
They would have understood the plea
For hidden in the message is:
'My Beloved come to Me.'
The 5 wise virgins heard this impassioned cry
….And answered 'Yes, my Beloved,
I am coming, it is I'
So they laid it all down
Living only to serve
The moral of the 10 virgins is:
Each got what they deserve.

Appendix 5 – The Bride of Christ

Who is the Bride of Christ? When asked this question, almost everyone answers, "the Church," or "the body of Christ," meaning all saved people. However, nowhere in the Bible is the Church called the Bride of Christ. The Church is called His body in Eph 1:22-23, but the body and the bride are not synonymous as has been supposed.

Using the "rule of first mention," and keeping in mind that the things written in the Old Testament are types and examples for our learning (Rom 15:4, 1Cr 10:11), we can see that the bride is taken out of the body. Two examples from the Old Testament illustrate this truth: The first bride Eve was not the body of Adam, but was taken out of his body. Adam is a type of Christ. Eve is a type for the bride.

In Gen 24 we have the story of Abraham who sent his servant to take a bride for his son, Isaac. Most people say this is a type for God the Father sending the Holy Spirit into the world for calling out the Church. However, this is not the true meaning of the story. While the Gospel is to go into all the world, in this story Abraham told the servant not to go to the Canaanites, but to go to his own people to take a bride for his son.

The correct interpretation is this: Abraham, a type of the Father, sent the servant, a type of the Holy Spirit, to his own people, a type of the Church, to take a bride for his son Isaac, a type of Christ. When the message of salvation goes forth, it goes to everyone; but when God calls for His bride, He calls not the world, but His own people, or His family.

Our Lord used the term "family" because of its meaning to us in our physical life. We are born the first time into a physical family. When we believe on the Lord Jesus Christ, trusting Him

Who died in our place, we are born again, into the family of God. The word "bride" is used in a similar sense. We know what the blessings of family life involve. We also know the bride and groom share a closeness and an intimacy, which is not shared by the other members of the family.

With these thoughts in mind, we can see how the Lord calls those who are His to come up closer. *"I beseech you therefore, brethren, by the mercies of God, that ye present your bodies a living sacrifice, holy, acceptable unto God which is your reasonable service. **And be not conformed to this world: but be ye transformed by the renewing of your mind**, that ye may prove what is that good and acceptable and perfect will of God"* (Rom 12:1-2).

Not many Christians heed this direct command. Many who are saved continue to conform to this world and they never experience sweet communion and fellowship with the Lord Jesus; and like Esau, forfeit spiritual rewards in the future for gratification of the carnal nature in the present.

In writing to the carnal Corinthians, Paul tells them they are espoused to one husband, that is, they are promised in marriage or engaged. The word espoused is a very similar word used in Mat 1:18, where Mary is espoused to Joseph. Before they came together he thought of putting her away since he thought she had been unfaithful. Many believers today may be unfaithful, and there is a sense in which the Lord may *"put them away."*

This does not mean the loss of their salvation, but in Rev 16:15, we read, *"Behold I come as a thief. Blessed is he that watcheth, and keepeth his garments lest he walk naked and they see his shame."* This refers not to His righteousness with which He clothes us for our own salvation (Isa 61:10), but to a garment of good works (deeds) which may be maintained with a profitable result, or which may be lost to our shame and loss of rewards when Jesus returns (1Jo 2:28, Tts 3:8, and 2Jo 1:8).

Rev 19:7 shows us the bride *"makes herself ready"* for her soon marriage by providing a garment of good deeds. Many Christians do not live for Christ after they are saved and they are not preparing themselves to meet the Bridegroom.

Paul compared the Christian life to a race where all run, but only one receives the **"prize"** (1 Cor. 9:24-27). Paul was fearful that he would become a *"castaway"* so he worked diligently to keep his body in subjection. In chapter three of Philippians, Paul talks about losing all things so that he might *"gain Christ."* He also says that he wants to *"know Him and the power of His resurrection, and the fellowship of His sufferings, being conformed to His death, if, by any means, I may attain to the resurrection from the dead"* (Phl 3:10-11 – NKJV).

The resurrection Paul is talking about in this passage of Scripture is something that is earned. It refers to a partial resurrection of Christians who have attained to a certain standard. Hebrews 11:35 calls it the *"better resurrection."* In the above passage of Scripture Paul emphasizes that he is working very hard to win the **"prize,"** which is in Christ Jesus. The prize is clearly the highest reward that a believer can receive for faithful, spirit-filled service in the Lord's work. The Scriptures are replete with types, parables and doctrinal statements that express the honor and blessing attached to those who are part of the wedding of the Lord Jesus Christ.

Rev 3:18 tells us to buy white raiment that we may be clothed and that the shame of our nakedness not appear. The white raiment is *"the righteous acts and deeds"* of the Saints. The word *"buy"* is used to show that it will cost the child of God to be among those who make up the Bride of Christ. A separated and surrendered life is costly, but how great will be the reward for those who dare to pay the price.

Many Christians are not doing these things, and may not be part of the bride. We will all give an account of our lives and be rewarded according to the good and bad we have done (please read 2Cr 5:10). Some do not live for the Lord and may suffer the loss of rewards. Those who have not provided themselves with a wedding garment may be spiritually naked and ashamed when the Lord returns.

Salvation is a free gift of God. It is eternal and cannot be lost. Crowns, rewards, and an inheritance into the Kingdom are based upon faithfulness to Him. To be part of the Bride of Christ is a great reward to those Christians who have paid the price. It is a figurative picture of those who have lived a clean, pure, and holy life yielded to Him.

Just as any bride would prepare herself for her earthly bridegroom, so should every Christian prepare themselves to meet their heavenly Bridegroom. Just as a bride would not wear blue jeans to her wedding, the Bride of Christ will not be an average lukewarm Christian (read the warning to the Church of Laodicea (Rev 3:14-22).

The Church is one body, made up of all believers in Christ. Some are spiritual and some are carnal (1Cr 3). As outlined in Appendix 4, some are wise and some are foolish. Who then is the bride?

Those who are providing themselves with a wedding garment and those who are preparing to meet the Bridegroom when He returns, as evidenced by their pure and sincere devotion to Jesus. All Christians will not qualify to be the bride. Will you?[1]

One of the main purposes of this book is to help you prepare for the great Wedding that is about to occur. Please visit our website for more help in preparing to meet the Bridegroom when He returns for His beloved bride.

Appendix 6 – The Song of Songs (CDG)

Christian David Ginsburg was a renowned Hebrew scholar and Biblical commentator. He was born in Warsaw, Poland on December 25, 1831 to orthodox Jewish parents. He became a Christian at age 15, and was connected with the Liverpool branch of the London Society's Mission to the Jews, but retired in 1863, devoting himself entirely to literary work. In 1857, he published his work on the Song of Songs, which he translated from the original Hebrew. He properly identifies the three primary characters as outlined in Appendix 2, and his commentary that is listed in the Bibliography is one of the finest works on this most difficult book of the Bible. Ginsburg's rendition of the Song is included in this Appendix, making it much easier for the reader to understand the great truth God has for us in this beautiful Song. The Song's drama will be presented in the following seven acts:

Act 1 – Love Between Two Lovers
Shulamite in royal tent separated from her beloved shepherd.
(Song of Songs 1:2 to 2:7)

THE SHULAMITE

2) Oh for a kiss of the kisses of his mouth! For sweet are thy caresses above wine. 3) Sweet is the odour of thy perfumes, Which perfume thou art, by thy name diffused abroad, Therefore do the damsels love-thee. 4) Oh draw me after thee! Oh let us flee together! The king has brought me into his apartments, But we exult and rejoice in thee, We praise thy love more than wine, The upright love thee. 5) I am swarthy, 0 ye daughters of Jerusalem, As the tents of Kedar, But comely as the pavilions of Solomon. 6) Disdain me not because I am dark, For the sun hath browned me. My mother's sons were severe with me, They made me keeper of their vineyards, Though my own vineyard I never kept.
7) Tell me, 0 thou whom my soul loveth, Where thou feedest thy flock, Where thou causest it to lie down at noon, Lest I should be roaming Among the flocks of thy companions.

DAUGHTERS OF JERUSALEM

8) If thou knowest not, 0 fairest among women, Go in the footsteps of the flocks, And feed thy kids By the tents of the shepherds.

SOLOMON

9) To my steed in the chariot of Pharaoh Do I compare thee, 0 my love. 10) Beautiful is thy countenance in the circlet, Thy neck in the necklace! 11) A golden circlet will we make thee, With studs of silver.

THE SHULAMITE

12) While the king is at his table My nard shall diffuse its fragrance. 13) A bag of myrrh resting in my bosom Is my beloved unto me. 14) A bunch of cypress-flowers from the garden of En-gedi Is my beloved unto me.

THE SHEPHERD

15) Behold, thou art beautiful, my love; Behold, thou art beautiful, Thine eyes are doves.

THE SHULAMITE

16) Behold, thou art comely, my beloved,
Yea thou art lovely;
Yea, verdant is our couch;
17) Our bower is of cedar arches,
Our retreat of cypress roof:

CHAPTER 2

1) I am a mere flower of the plain,
A lily of the valley.

THE SHEPHERD

2) As a lily among the thorns,
So is my loved one among the damsels.

THE SHULAMITE

3) As an apple-tree among the wild trees, So is my beloved
among the youths. I delight to sit beneath its shade,
For delicious is its fruit to my taste.
4) He led me into that bower of delight,
And overshaded me with love.
5) Oh, strengthen me with grape-cakes,
Refresh me with apples, For I am sick with love!
6) Let his left hand be under my head,
And his right hand support me!

7) I adjure you,
0 ye daughters of Jerusalem,
By the gazelles, or the hinds of the field,
Neither to excite nor to incite my affection
Till it wishes another love.
(Sgs 1:2 to 2:7 – CDG)

Act 2 – Longing During Separation
Shulamite longs to be reunited with her beloved.
(Song of Songs 2:8-17)

THE SHULAMITE
8) Hark! my beloved! Lo, he came
Leaping over the mountains, Bounding over the hills.
9) My beloved was like a gazelle, Or the young one of a hind.
Lo! there he stood behind our wall,
He looked through the window,
He glanced through the lattice.
10) My beloved spake, he spake to me,
"Arise, my love, my fair one, and come!
11) For lo, the winter is past, The rain is over, is gone.
12) The flowers appear upon the fields,
The time of singing is come,
The cooing of the turtle-dove is heard in our land.
13) The fig-tree sweetens her green figs, The vines blossom,
They diffuse fragrance;
Arise, my love, my fair one, and come!
14) My dove in the clefts of the rock, In the hiding-place of the
cliff, Let me see thy countenance,
Let me hear thy voice, For sweet is thy voice,
And thy countenance lovely."
THE BROTHERS OF THE SHULAMITE
15) Catch us the foxes, the little foxes
Which destroy the vineyards,
For our vineyards are in bloom.
THE SHULAMITE
16) My beloved is mine, and I am his,
His who feeds his flock among the lilies.
17) When the day cools, And the shadows flee away,
Return, haste, 0 my beloved,
Like the gazelle or the young one of the hind,
Over the mountains of separation.
(Sgs 2:8 to 2:17 – CDG)

Act 3 – Dream for Soulmate
Shulamite dreams of being with her beloved shepherd.
(Song of Songs 3:1-5)

CHAPTER 3

1) When on my nightly couch,
I still sought him whom my soul loveth;
I sought him, but found him not.
2) I must arise now and go about the city,
In the streets and in the squares;
I must seek him whom my soul loveth:
I sought him, but found him not.
3) The watchmen who patrol the city found me:
"Have you seen him whom my soul loveth?"

4) Scarcely had I passed them,
When I found him whom my soul loveth;
I seized him and would not let him go
Till I brought him to the house of my mother,
Into the apartment of her who gave me birth.

5) I adjure you, 0 ye daughters of Jerusalem,
By the gazelles By the hinds of the field,
Neither to excite nor to incite my affection
Till it wishes another love.
(Sgs 3:1 to 3:5 – CDG)

Act 4 – Offer to Rescue
Her shepherd lover offers to rescue his Shulamite after she was
taken to Solomon's royal palace in Jerusalem.
(Song of Songs 3:6 to 5:1)

ONE OF THE INHABITANTS OF JERUSALEM
6) What is that coming up from the country,
As in columns of smoke,
Perfumed with myrrh, with frankincense,
And all sorts of aromatics from the merchants?

ANOTHER [INHABITANT]
7) Lo! it is the palanquin of Solomon, Around it are threescore
valiant men From the valiant of Israel:
8) All skilled in the sword, expert in war,
Each with his sword girded on his thigh
Against the nightly marauders.

A THIRD
9) A palanquin hath king Solomon made for himself,
Of the wood of Lebanon.
10) Its pillars he hath made of silver,
Its support of gold, its seat of purple,
Its interior tesselated most lovely
By the daughters of Jerusalem.

A FOURTH
11) Come out, ye daughters of Zion, And behold King Solomon;
The crown with which his mother crowned him
On the day of his espousals, On the day of his gladness of heart.
(Sgs 3:6 to 3:11 – CDG)

THE SHEPHERD, ADVANCING TO THE SHULAMITE
CHAPTER 4
1) Behold, thou art beautiful, my loved one,
Behold, thou art beautiful!
Thine eyes are doves behind thy veil
Thy hair is like a flock of goats, Springing down Mount Gilead.

2) Thy teeth are like a flock of sheep
Which come up from the washing-pool,
All of which are paired,
And not one among them is bereaved.
3) Like a braid of scarlet are thy lips,
And thy mouth is lovely:
Like a part of the pomegranate
Are thy cheeks behind thy veil;
4) Thy neck is like the tower of David,
Reared for the builder's model:
A thousand shields are hung upon it,
All sorts of bucklers of the mighty.
5) Thy bosom like two young fawns,
Twins of a gazelle, feeding among lilies.

THE SHULAMITE
6) When the day cools
And the shadows flee away,
I will go to the mount of myrrh, To the hill of frankincense.

THE SHEPHERD
7) Thou art all beautiful, my loved one,
And there is no blemish in thee.
8) with me, with me, my betrothed Thou shalt go from Lebanon;
Thou shalt go from the heights of Amann, From the summit of
Shenir and Hennon, From the habitations of lions,
From the mountains of panthers.
9) Thou hast emboldened me, My sister, my betrothed,
Thou hast emboldened me,
With one of thine eyes,
With one of the chains of thy neck .
10) How sweet is thy love, 0 my sister, my betrothed!
How sweet is thy love above wine!
And the fragrance of thy perfumes above all the spices!
11) Thy lips, 0 my betrothed, distil honey:
Honey and milk are under thy tongue,

Act 4 – Offer to Rescue (continued)

And the odour of thy garments is as the smell of Lebanon.
12) A closed garden art thou, my sister, my betrothed,
A closed garden, a sealed fountain.
13) Thy shoots like a garden of pomegranates,
With precious fruits, Cypresses and nards,
14) Nard and crocus, Calamus and cinnamon,
with all sorts of frankincense trees,
Myrrh and aloes;
15) With all kinds of excellent aromatics,
With a garden-fountain,
A well of living waters,
And streams flowing from Lebanon.
16) Arise, 0 north wind! and come, thou south!
Blow upon my garden,
That its perfumes may flow out!

THE SHULAMITE

16) Let my beloved come into his garden
And eat its delicious fruits!
(Sgs 4:1 to 4:16 – CDG)

CHAPTER 5

THE SHEPHERD

1) I am coming into my garden, my sister,
my betrothed: I am gathering my myrrh with my spices,
I am eating my honeycomb with my honey,
I am drinking my wine with my milk.

SOME OF THE DAUGHTERS OF JERUSALEM

Eat, 0 friends!
Drink, and drink abundantly, 0 beloved!
(Sgs 5:1 – CDG)

Act 5 – Dream of Separation
Shulamite dreams again and tells the daughters of Jerusalem
about her dream of her shepherd lover.
(Song of Songs 5:2 to 5:8)

THE SHULAMITE
2) I was sleeping, but my heart kept awake,
Hark! my beloved! he is knocking!
Open to me, my sister, my love!
My dove, my perfect beauty!
For my head is filled with dew,
My locks with the drops of the night.
3) I have put off my tunic,
How shall I put it on?
I have washed my feet,
How shall I soil them?
4) My beloved withdrew his hand from the door hole,
And my heart was disquieted within me.
5) I immediately arose to open to my beloved,
And my hands dropped with myrrh,
And my fingers with liquid myrrh,
Upon the handles of the bolt.
6) I opened to my beloved,
But my beloved had withdrawn, was gone!
My soul departed when he spoke of it!
I sought him, and found him not;
I called him, and he answered me not.
7) The watchmen who patrol the city found me:
They beat me, they wounded me;
The keepers of the walls stripped me of my veiling garment.

8) I adjure you, 0 ye daughters of Jerusalem,
If ye shall find my beloved,
What will ye tell him?
Tell him that I am sick of love.
(Sgs 5:2 to 5:8 – CDG)

Act 6 – Longing for Her Lover

She tells the daughters of Jerusalem all about her shepherd
lover but Solomon interrupts and tries to allure her to him.
She refuses the king because she is espoused to her lover.
(Song of Songs 5:9 to 8:4)

DAUGHTERS OF JERUSALEM

9) What is thy beloved more than another beloved,
0 thou fairest among women?
What is thy beloved, more than another beloved,
That thou thus adjurest us?

THE SHULAMITE

10) My beloved is white and ruddy, Distinguished above
thousands; 11) His head is as the finest gold,
His flowing locks are black as the raven.
12) His eyes, like doves in water streams,
Are bathing in milk, sitting on fulness;
13) His cheeks are like beds of balsam,
Elevations of aromatic plants;
His lips are like lilies distilling liquid myrrh.
14) His hands like golden cylinders, inlaid with chrysolite,
His body is like polished ivory, covered with sapphires.
15) His legs are like pillars of marble
Based upon pedestals of gold.
His aspect is like that of Lebanon.
He is distinguished as the cedars.
16) His voice is exquisitely sweet;
Yea, his whole person is exceedingly lovely.
Such is my beloved, such my friend, 0 daughters of Jerusalem.

DAUGHTERS OF JERUSALEM

CHAPTER 6

1) Whither is thy beloved gone, 0 thou fairest among women?
Whither is thy beloved turned away?
Say, that we may seek him with thee.

THE SHULAMITE

2) My beloved is gone down into his garden,
To the beds of aromatics,
To feed in the gardens, and to gather lilies.
3) I am my beloved's, and my beloved is mine;
He who feeds his flock Among the lilies.

SOLOMON

4) Graceful art thou, O my love, as Tirzah, Beautiful as
Jerusalem, Awe-inspiring as bannered hosts!
5) Turn away thine eyes from me,
For they inspire me with awe! Thy hair is like a flock of goats
Springing down Mount Gilead;
6) Thy teeth are like a flock of sheep, Which come up from the
washing-pool; All of which are paired,
And not one among them is bereaved.
7) Like a part of the pomegranate
Are thy cheeks behind thy veil.
8) I have threescore queens, And fourscore concubines,
And maidens without number;
9) But she is my only one, my dove, my perfect beauty,
She, the delight of her mother,
She, the darling of her parent!
The damsels saw her and praised her
The queens also, and the concubines, and extolled her thus:
10) "Who is she that looks forth as the morn,
Beautiful as the moon, bright as the sun,
Awe-inspiring as bannered hosts?"

THE SHULAMITE

11) I went down into the nut-garden,
To look among the green plants by the river,
To see whether the vine was budding,
Whether the pomegranates were in bloom.
12) Unwittingly had my longing soul brought me
To the chariots of the companions of the prince.
(She goes away).

Act 6 – Longing for Her Lover (continued)

SOLOMON

13)*** *Return, return, 0 Shulamite,*
Return, return, that we may look at thee.

THE SHULAMITE

What will you behold in the Shulamite?

SOLOMON

Like a dance to double choirs.
(Sgs 5:9 to 6:13 –CDG)

CHAPTER 7

2) How beautiful are thy feet in sandals, 0 noble maiden!
The circuits of thy thighs like ornaments,
The work of a master's hands.
3) Thy navel is like a round goblet,
Let not spiced wine be wanted in it;
Thy body is like a heap of wheat, Hedged round with lilies.
4) Thy bosom is like two young fawns, Twins of a gazelle.
5) Thy neck is like an ivory tower;
Thine eyes are as the pools in Heshbon, By the populous gate;
Thy nose is as the tower of Lebanon,
Looking towards Damascus.
6) Thy head upon thee as purple,
And the tresses of thy head as crimson.
The king is captivated by the ringlets:
How beautiful and how charming,
0 love, in thy fascinations!
7) This thy growth is like a palm-tree,
And thy bosom like its clusters. 8)I long to climb this palm-tree,
I long to clasp its branches. May thy bosom be unto me
As the clusters of the vine, And the odour
of thy breath As that of apples;
9) And thy speech as delicious wine,
Which to my friend flows down with mellowed sweetness,
And causes slumbering lips to speak.

THE SHULAMITE
10) I belong to my beloved,
And it is for me to desire him.
11) Come, my beloved,
let us go into the country, Let us abide in the villages.
12) We will go early to the vineyards,
We will see whether the vine flourishes;
Whether the buds open;
Whether the pomegranates blossom;
There will I give thee my love.
13) The mandrakes diffuse fragrance,
And at our door are all sorts of delicious fruit,
Both new and old;
I have reserved them, 0 my beloved, for thee!

CHAPTER 8
1) Oh that thou wert as my brother,
As one who had been nourished in the bosom of my mother!
If I found thee in the street I would kiss thee,
And should no more be reproached.
2) I would lead thee thence,
I would bring thee into the house of my mother;
Thou shouldst be my teacher,
I would cause thee to drink Of the aromatic wine,
Of my pomegranate juice.
3) Let his left hand be under my head,
And his right hand support me!

4) I adjure you, 0 daughters of Jerusalem,
Neither to incite nor to excite my affection
Till it desires another love.
(Sgs 7:2 to 8:4 – CDG)

*** The original Hebrew and Greek text place verse 13 as the first verse of the next chapter (i.e., 7^1). Most English versions place this verse as the last verse in the chapter (i.e., 6^{13}). The numbering of the English versions is followed in this writing, although Ginsburg placed it as verse 1 of chapter 7.

Act 7 – Reunited With Her Beloved
Shulamite and her beloved shepherd reminisce where they
first fell in love and their blessed story of love.
(Song of Songs 8:5 to 8:14)

THE COMPANIONS OF THE SHEPHERD
5) Who is it that comes up from the plain,
Leaning upon her beloved?

THE SHULAMITE
Under this apple-tree I won thy heart,
Here thy mother travailed,
Here labouring she gave thee birth.

6) Oh, place me as a seal upon thy heart,
As a seal upon thine band!
For love is strong as death,
Affection as inexorable as Hades.
Its flames are flames of fire,
The flames of the Eternal.
7) Floods cannot quench love;
Streams cannot sweep it away.
If one should offer all his wealth for love,
He would be utterly despised.

ONE OF THE BROTHERS OF THE SHULAMITE
8) Our sister is still young,
And is not yet marriageable.
What shall we do for our sister,
When she shall be demanded in marriage?

ANOTHER BROTHER
9) If she be like a wall,
We will build upon her a silver turret.
But if she be like a door,
We will enclose her with boards of cedar.

THE SHULAMITE
10) I am like a wall,
And my bosom is as towers!
Then I was in his eyes
As one that findeth favour.

11) Solomon had a vineyard in Baal-hammon;
He let out the vineyard to tenants;
Each of whom yielded for the fruit of it
A thousand shekels of silver.
12) I will keep my own vineyard:
Be the thousands thine, 0 Solomon,
And the two hundreds to the keepers of its fruit!

THE SHEPHERD
13) 0 thou that dwellest in the gardens,
My companions are listening to thy voice,
Let me hear thy voice!

THE SHULAMITE
14) Haste, 0 my beloved,
And be like the gazelle,
as the young one of the hind,
Over the mountains of spices.
(Sgs 8:5 to 8:14 – CDG)

AN EXPOSITION OF THE SONG OF SOLOMON
By Matthew Henry

"All scripture, we are sure, is given by inspiration of God, and is profitable for the support and advancement of the interests of his kingdom among men, and it is never the less so for there being found in it some things dark and hard to be understood, which those that are unlearned and unstable wrest to their own destruction. . .

This book it appears to be a very bright and powerful ray of heavenly light, admirable fitted to excite pious and devout affections in holy souls, to draw out their desires towards God, to increase their delight in him, and improve their acquaintance and communion with him. It is an allegory, the letter of which kills those who rest in that and look no further, but the spirit of which gives life...It is a parable, which makes divine things more difficult to those who do not love them, but more plain and pleasant to those who do...Experienced Christians here find a counterpart of their experiences, and to them it is intelligible, while those neither understand it nor relish it who have no part nor lot in the matter. . .

The best key to this book is the 45th Psalm, which we find applied to Christ in the New Testament, and therefore this ought to be so too. It requires some pains to find out what may, probably, be the meaning of the Holy Spirit in the several parts of this book; as David's songs are many of them level to the capacity of the meanest, and there are shallows in them learned, and there are depths in it in which an elephant may swim. But, when the meaning is found out, it will be of admirable use to excite pious and devout affections in us; and the same truths which are plainly laid down in other scriptures when they are extracted out of this come to the soul with a more pleasing power." (Excerpt from the Preface)

Appendix 7 – Signs of Christ's Coming

As described earlier in this beautiful Song of Songs (please see p. 28), our beloved Shepherd is calling His faithful to come away with Him at the time when we see the fig tree begin to bud: *"putteth forth her green figs"* (Sgs 2^{13}). Modern Bible teachers and students believe that the rebirth of the nation of Israel represents the budding of the *fig tree* that Jesus described to His disciples as he sat on the Mount of Olives, and we are living in the generation that won't pass away before He returns.

*"Verily I say unto you, This generation shall not pass,
till all these things be fulfilled"* (Mat 24:34).

With Israel becoming a nation in 1948, we have been alerted that the Lord's return is fast approaching. Jesus also told his disciples a second sign to look for in the parable of Noah:

*"As it was in the days of Noah,
so it will be at the coming of the Son of Man."*
(Mat 24:37 – NIV)

Here the Lord is telling the Church that just prior to his return, things will be the same as they were back in Noah's day. This pictures life going on right up until the day that the rapture occurs, and the judgments of God are suddenly released upon the earth. A careful study of Genesis 6 will alert the reader to the fact that living in these end times is almost parallel to the time before the flood. The world has become a great cesspool of corruption, violence, sex, drugs, idolatry, witchcraft and other perversions. Reading the account in Genesis is like reading today's newspaper or listening to the daily news.

In the Lord's parable concerning Noah, Jesus was also giving us a second important sign that His return is drawing very near.

Sign of Christ's Coming

April 8, 1997

Comet Hale-Bopp Over New York City
Credit and Copyright: J. Sivo
http://antwrp.gsfc.nasa.gov/apod/ap970408.html
"What's that point of light above the World Trade Center? It's Comet Hale-Bopp! Both faster than a speeding bullet and able to "leap" tall buildings in its single orbit, Comet Hale-Bopp is also bright enough to be seen even over the glowing lights of one of the world's premier cities. In the foreground lies the East River, while much of New York City's Lower Manhattan can be seen between the river and the comet."

"But as the days of Noe were, so shall also the coming of the Son of man be. For as in the days that were before the flood they were eating and drinking, marrying and giving in marriage, until the day that Noe entered into the ark, And knew not until the flood came, and took them all away; so shall also the coming of the Son of man be."
(Mat 24:37-39)

These words from our wonderful Lord have several applications about the generation that is about to witness the Lord's return.

Seas Lifted Up

Throughout the Old Testament, the time of the coming Tribulation period is described as the time when the "seas have lifted up," and also as coming in as a "flood" (please see Jeremiah 51:42, Hosea 5:10, Daniel 11:40 and Psalm 93:3-4 for just a few examples).

This is a direct parallel to the time of Noah when the Great Flood of water came to wipe out every living creature, except for righteous Noah and his family, and the pairs of animals that God spared. While God said that He would never flood the earth again with water, the coming Judgement will be by fire (see II Peter 3:10). The book of Revelation shows that billions of people are about to perish in the terrible time that lies just ahead (see Revelation 6:8 and 9:15).

2 Witnesses

A guiding principle of God is to establish a matter based upon the witness of two or more:

> "...a matter must be established by the testimony of two or three witnesses" (Deuteronomy 19:15 – NIV).

In 1994, God was able to get the attention of mankind when Comet Shoemaker-Levy crashed into Jupiter on the 9th of Av (on the Jewish calendar). Interestingly, this Comet was named after the "two" witnesses who first discovered it.

In 1995, "two" more astronomers also discovered another comet. It was called Comet Hale-Bopp and it reached its closest approach to planet Earth on March 23, 1997. It has been labeled as the most widely viewed comet in the history of mankind.

Scientists have determined that Comet Hale-Bopp's orbit brought it to our solar system 4,465 years ago (see Notes 1 and 2 below). In other words, the comet made its appearance near Earth in 1997 and also in 2468 BC. Remarkably, this comet preceded the Great Flood by 120 years! God warned Noah of this in Genesis 6:3:

> *"My Spirit shall not strive with man forever, for he is indeed flesh; yet his days shall be one hundred and twenty years."*

Days of Noah
What does all of this have to do with the Lord's return? Noah was born around 2948 BC, and Genesis 7:11, tells us that the Flood took place when Noah was 600, or in 2348 BC.

Remember, our Lord told us: ***"As it was in the days of Noah, so it will be at the coming of the Son of Man"*** (Matthew 24:37 – NIV).

In the original Greek, it is saying: *"exactly like"* it was, so it will be when He comes (see Strong's #5618).

During the days of Noah, Comet Hale-Bopp arrived on the scene as a harbinger of the Great Flood. Just as this same comet appeared before the Flood, could its arrival again in 1997 be a sign that God's final Judgement, also known as the time of great tribulation, is about to begin?

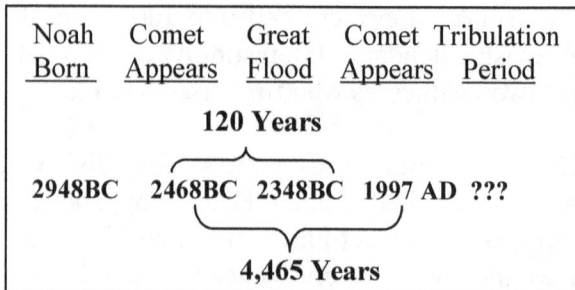

Noah Born	Comet Appears	Great Flood	Comet Appears	Tribulation Period
		120 Years		
2948BC	2468BC	2348BC	1997 AD	???
		4,465 Years		

Comet Hale-Bopp arrived 120 years before the Flood as a warning to mankind. Only righteous Noah heeded God's warning and built the ark, as God instructed. By faith, Noah was obedient to God and, as a result, saved himself and his family from destruction.

Remember, Jesus told us His return would be preceded by great heavenly signs: *"And there shall be signs in the sun, and in the moon, and in the stars; and upon the earth distress of nations, with perplexity; the sea and the waves roaring..."* (Luke 21:25)

Just as this large comet appeared as a 120-year warning to Noah, its arrival in 1997 tells us that Jesus is getting ready to return again. Is this the **"Sign"** Jesus referred to?

Jesus was asked 3 questions by the disciples:
"Tell us, (1) when shall these things be" (the destruction of the city of Jerusalem), *" and (2) what shall be the **sign** of thy coming, and (3) of the end of the world?"* (Matthew 24:3)

Sign of Christ's Coming

The **first** question had to do with events that were fulfilled in 70 AD. The **third** question has to do with the future time at the very end of the age.

The **second** question, however, has to do with the time of Christ's second coming. Jesus answered this second question in His description of the days of Noah found in Matthew 24:33-39:

*(33) "So likewise ye, when ye shall see all these things, know that it is near, even at the doors. (34) Verily I say unto you, This generation shall not pass, till all these things be fulfilled. (35) Heaven and earth shall pass away, but my words shall not pass away. (36) But of that day and hour knoweth no man, no, not the angels of heaven, but my Father only. (37) **But as the days of Noe were, so shall also the coming of the Son***

of man be. *(38)For as in the days that were before the flood they were eating and drinking, marrying and giving in marriage, until the day that Noe entered into the ark, (39) And knew not until the flood came, and took them all away; so shall also the coming of the Son of man be."*

Jesus is telling us that the **sign** of His coming will be as it was during the days of Noah. As Comet Hale-Bopp was a sign to the people in Noah's day, its arrival in 1997 may be a sign that Jesus is coming back again soon. Comet Hale-Bopp could be the very sign Jesus was referring to, which would announce His return for His faithful.

Remember, Jesus said, *"**exactly as** it was in the days of Noah, so will it be when He returns."* The appearance of Comet Hale-Bopp in 1997 is a strong indication that the tribulation period is about to begin, but before then, Jesus is coming for His bride!

Keep looking up! Jesus is coming again very soon!
As Noah prepared for the destruction God warned him approximately 120 years before the Flood, Jesus has given mankind final warnings that we are living in the generation that will witness His return. We do not know how long a generation may be. For this reason we need to be wise like Noah and prepare by always remembering our Lord's instructions:

Watch and Pray

*"(34)And take heed to yourselves, lest at any time your hearts be overcharged with surfeiting, and drunkenness, and cares of this life, and so that day come upon you unawares. (35) For as a snare shall it come on all them that dwell on the face of the whole earth. (36) **Watch ye therefore, and pray always, that ye may be accounted worthy to escape all these things that shall come to pass, and to stand before the Son of man"** (Luke 21:34-36).*

Footnotes to Appendix 7

(1) The original orbit of Comet Hale-Bopp was calculated to be approximately 265 years by engineer George Sanctuary in his article, *Three Craters In Israel*, published on 3/31/01 found at: http://www.gsanctuary.com/3craters.html#3c_r13

Comet Hale-Bopp's orbit around the time of the Flood changed from 265 years to about 4,200 years. Because the plane of the comet's orbit is perpendicular to the earth's orbital plane (ecliptic), Mr. Sanctuary noted: "A negative time increment was used for this simulation...to back the comet away from the earth.... past Jupiter... and then out of the solar system. The simulation suggests that the past-past orbit had a very eccentric orbit with a period of only 265 years. When the comet passed Jupiter (*around 2203BC*) its orbit was deflected upward, coming down near the earth 15 months later with the comet's period changed from 265 years to about (*4,200*) years." (*added text for clarity*)

(2) Don Yeomans, with NASA's Jet Propulsion Laboratory, made the following observations regarding the comet's orbit: "By integrating the above orbit forward and backward in time until the comet leaves the planetary system and then referring the osculating orbital elements...the following orbital periods result:

Original orbital period before entering planetary system = 4200 years. Future orbital period after exiting the planetary system = 2380 years."

This analysis can be found at:

http://www2.jpl.nasa.gov/comet/ephemjpl6.html

Based upon the above two calculations we have the following:

265 [a] + 4,200 [b] = 4,465 Years

1997 AD – 4,465 Years = 2468 BC = Hale Bopp arrived

(a) Orbit period calculated by George Sanctuary before deflection around 2203 BC.

(b) Orbit period calculated by Don Yeomans after 1997 visit.

Tract Included In Appendix 7

This tract was written in 1997 when Comet Hale-Bopp entered our solar system. In 2017 it will be 20 years from the time of its appearance, which is also 50 years from the time the City of Jerusalem was recaptured by Israel (1967). According to Bullinger, "Fifty is the number of jubilee or deliverance, pointing to rest following on as the result of the perfect consummation of time" (Bullinger, p. 268).

A Prayer By the Bride

*FATHER GOD in Heaven
We want to be Seekers of
Your Heart in Spirit and in Truth
All the Days of our Life.
Purify our hearts and lives
So we will be pleasing to You
In all of our ways. We want to be
Soft and pliant clay in
Your Hands so you can form
us into the Image of Your SON.
Prepare us for Your soon
Coming so we can stand
Before You blameless
And unashamed when our
Time comes. Without You
We can do nothing, but sheltered
Under Your Wings, we can do
All things. Help us all in the
Mighty Name of JESUS.
His Majesty and our
Coming King.*

Amen

Special Invitation

This book hopes to inspire you to know and love Jesus Christ. If you have never been saved before, would you like to be saved? The Bible shows that it's simple to be saved...

- **Realize you are a sinner.**
  "As it is written, There is none righteous, no, not one:"
  (Romans 3:10)
  "... for there is no difference. For all have sinned, and come short of the glory of God;" (Romans 3:22-23)
- **Realize you CAN NOT save yourself.**
  "But we are all as an unclean thing, and all our righteousness are as filthy rags; ..." (Isaiah 64:6)
  "Not by works of righteousness which we have done, but according to his mercy he saved us, ..." (Titus 3:5)
- **Realize that Jesus Christ died on the cross to pay for your sins.**
  "Who his own self bare our sins in his own body on the tree,..." (I Peter 2:24)
  "... Unto him that loved us, and washed us from our sins in his own blood," (Revelation 1:5)
- **Simply by faith receive Jesus Christ as your personal Savior.**
  "But as many as received him, to them gave he power to become the sons of God, even to them that believe on his name:" (John 1:12)
  " ...Sirs, what must I do to be saved? And they said, Believe on the Lord Jesus Christ, and thou shalt be saved, and thy house." (Acts 16:30-31)
  "...if you confess with your mouth, 'Jesus is Lord,' and believe in your heart God raised him from the dead, you will be saved." (Romans 10:9 – NIV)

WOULD YOU LIKE TO BE SAVED?

If you would like to be saved, believe on the Lord Jesus Christ (Acts 16:31) right now by making the following confession of faith:

> Lord Jesus, I know that I am a sinner, and unless you save me, I am lost. I thank you for dying for me at Calvary. By faith I come to you now, Lord, the best way I know how, and ask you to save me. I believe that God raised you from the dead and acknowledge you as my personal Saviour.

If you believed on the Lord, this is the most important decision of your life. You are now saved by the precious blood of Jesus Christ, which was shed for you and your sins. Now that you have believed on Jesus as your personal Saviour, you will want to find a Church where you can be baptized as your first act of obedience, and where the Word of God is taught so you can continue to grow in your faith. Ask the Holy Spirit to help you as you read the Bible to learn all that God has for your life.

Also, see the Reference Notes and Bibliography section of this book, where you will find recommended books and websites that will help you on your wonderful journey.

Endtimes
The Bible indicates that we are living in the final days and Jesus Christ is getting ready to return very soon. This book was written to help people prepare to meet the beloved Shepherd when He comes. The word of God indicates that the tribulation period is rapidly approaching and that the Antichrist is getting ready to emerge on the world scene.

Jesus promised His disciples that there is a way to escape the horrible time of testing and persecution that will soon devastate this planet. One of the purposes of this book is to help you get prepared so you will be ready when Jesus Christ returns.

About The Author

Jim Harman has been a Christian for 38 years. He has diligently studied the Word of God with a particular emphasis on Prophecy. Jim has written several books and the most essential titles are available at www.ProphecyCountdown.com: ***The Coming Spiritual Earthquake, The Kingdom, Overcomers' Guide To The Kingdom, and Calling All Overcomers.*** All of these books may be freely downloaded as PDF files and they will encourage you to continue *"Looking"* for the blessed hope of the Lord's soon return.

Jim's professional experience included being a Certified Public Accountant (CPA) and a Certified Property Manager (CPM). He had an extensive background in both public accounting and financial management with several well-known national firms.

Jim has been fortunate to have been acquainted with several mature believers who understand and teach the deeper truths of the Bible. It is Jim's strong desire that many will come to realize the importance of seeking the Kingdom and seeking Christ's righteousness as we approach the soon return of our Lord and Saviour Jesus Christ.

The burden of his heart is to see many come to know the joy of Christ's triumph in their life as they become true overcomers; qualified and ready to rule and reign with Christ in the coming Kingdom.

To contact the author for questions, to arrange for speaking engagements or to order multiple copies of this book:

Jim Harman
P.O. Box 941612
Maitland, FL 32794
JamesTHarman@aol.com

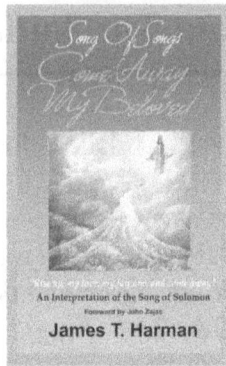

Song Of Songs
Come Away My Beloved

An Interpretation of the Song of Solomon
Foreword by John Zajac

James T. Harman

God placed the Song of Solomon in the heart of the Bible for a special reason. ***Come Away My Beloved*** helps reveal that reason in a most enchanting way. In this refreshing commentary you will realize why this ancient love story has perplexed Bible students and commentators down through the ages.

Find out the prophetic importance veiled within the Song's poetic imagery and experience a renewed love for the Lord as you explore one of the most passionate love stories of all time.

Witness the wonderful joys of romance and devotion shared by two young lovers. Discover enduring lessons of virtue and faithfulness, and learn amazing truths that have been hidden within the greatest love Song ever written.

Written almost 3,000 years ago this brilliant Song of love reflects God's desire for every man and woman; not only in their present lives but also in their relationship with Him.

This book will revive your heart with a fervent love for your Saviour. It will also help you prepare for your glorious wedding day when Jesus returns for His devoted bride.

Allow this beautiful story of love and passion to ignite a flame in your heart and let this inspirational Song arouse your heart to join in the impassioned cry with the rest of the bride:

"Make haste, my beloved, and come quickly…"

Download your FREE copy: www.ProphecyCountdown.com

Or from Amazon.com – Available in Paperback and or Kindle Edition

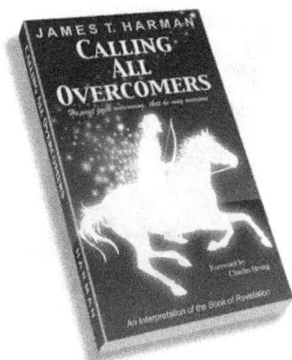

Perplexed by the book of Revelation? Not sure what all the signs, symbols and metaphors really mean? Jim Harman's latest work unravels Apostle John's remarkable revelation of Jesus Christ and what's in store for the inhabitants of planet Earth. This extraordinary commentary is not another cookie-cutter rehash of the popular teachings fostered by the *Left Behind* phenomena so prevalent in today's church.

One of the central messages in the book of Revelation is that God is calling men to be genuine overcomers. Jesus Christ has been sent out from the throne of God to conquer men's hearts so they can also be overcomers.

The purpose of this book is to encourage people to embrace him as the King of their heart and allow his life to reign in theirs. He wants you to be able to overcome by his mighty power and strength living inside of you just as He overcame for all of us. Jesus will be looking for a faithful remnant qualified to rule and reign with him when he returns. This book will help you prepare to be the overcomer Jesus will be looking for.

The reader will come away with a new and enlightened understanding of what the last book in God's Word is all about. Understand the book of Revelation and why it is so important for believers living in the last days of the Church age.

Download your FREE copy: www.ProphecyCountdown.com

Or from Amazon.com – Available in Paperback and or Kindle Edition

Once a person is saved, the number one priority should be seeking entrance into the Kingdom through the salvation of their soul. It is pictured as a runner in a race seeking a prize represented by a crown that will last forever.

The salvation of the soul and entrance into the coming Kingdom are only achieved through much testing and the trial of one's faith. If you are going through difficulty, then REJOICE:

> *"Blessed is the man who perseveres under trial, because when he has stood the test, he will receive the crown of life that God has promised to those who love Him."* (James 1:12)

The "Traditional" teaching on the "THE KINGDOM" has taken the Church captive into believing all Christians will rule and reign with Christ no matter if they have lived faithful and obedient lives, or if they have been slothful and disobedient with the talents God has given them. Find out the important Truth before Jesus Christ returns.

MUST READING FOR EVERY CHRISTIAN

Jesus Christ is returning for His faithful overcoming followers. Don't miss the opportunity of ruling and reigning with Christ in the coming KINGDOM!

Download your FREE copy: www.ProphecyCountdown.com

Or from Amazon.com – Available in Paperback and or Kindle Edition

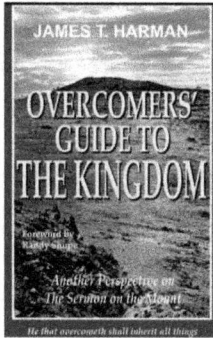

Get ready to climb back up the Mountain to listen to Christ's teachings once again. Though you may have read this great Sermon on the Mount many times, discover exciting promises that many have missed.

The purpose of this book is to help Christians be the Overcomers that Jesus wants them to be and to help them gain their own entrance in the coming Kingdom. Learn what seeking the Kingdom of God is all about and be among the chosen few who will "enter into" the coming Kingdom. *"Whoever hears these sayings of Mine, and does them, I will liken him to a wise man who built his house upon the rock."* (Mat 7:24)

Also learn about:
- The link between Beatitudes and Fruit of the Spirit
- What the "law of Christ" really is
- The critical importance of the "Lord's prayer"
- How to be an Overcomer
- THE SIGN of Christ's soon Coming
- A new song entitled: LOOKING FOR THE SON which has the message of how vitally important it is to be Watching for the Lord's return and the consequences to those who are not looking.

Download your FREE copy: www.ProphecyCountdown.com

Or from Amazon.com – Available in Paperback and or Kindle Edition

LOOKING FOR THE SON
Lyrics by Jim Harman
Can be sung to the hit tune: *"ROLLING IN THE DEEP"*

Lyric	Scripture
There's a fire burning in my heart	Luke 24:32
Yearning for the Lord to come,	Rev. 22:17, Mat. 6:33
and His Kingdom come to start	
Soon He'll come.....so enter the narrow gate	Lk. 21:34-36,Mat.7:13
Even though you mock me now...	II Peter 3:4
He'll come to set things straight	
Watch how I'll leave in the twinkling of an eye	I Corinthians 15:52
Don't be surprised when I go up in the sky	Revelation 3:10
There's a fire burning in my heart	Luke 24:32
Yearning for my precious Lord	Revelation 22:17
And His Kingdom come to start	Revelation 20:4-6
Your love of this world, has forsaken His	I John 2:15
It leaves me knowing that you could have had it all	Revelation 21:7
Your love of this world, was oh so reckless	Revelation 3:14-22
I can't help thinking	Philippians 1:3-6
You would have had it all	Revelation 21:7
Looking for the Son	Titus 2:13, Luke 21:36
(Tears are gonna fall, not looking for the Son)	Matthew 25:10-13
You had His holy Word in your hand	II Timothy 3:16
(You're gonna wish you had listened to me)	Jeremiah 25:4-8
And you missed it...for your self	Matthew 22:11-14
(Tears are gonna fall, not looking for the Son)	Matthew 25:10-13
Brother, I have a story to be told	Habakkuk 2:2
It's the only one that's true	John 3:16-17
And it should've made your heart turn	II Peter 3:9
Remember me when I rise up in the air	I Corinthians 15:52
Leaving your home down here	I Corinthians 15:52
For true Treasures beyond compare	Matthew 6:20
Your love of this world, has forsaken His	I John 2:15
It leaves me knowing that you could have had it all	Revelation 21:7
Your love of this world, was oh so reckless	Revelation 3:14-22
I can't help thinking	Philippians 1:3-6
You would have had it all	Revelation 21:7

(Lyrics in parentheses represent background vocals)
(CONTINUED)

© Copyright 2011-16, Prophecy Countdown Publications, LLC

Lyric	Scripture
Looking for the Son	Titus 2:13, Lk. 21:36
(Tears are gonna fall, not looking for the Son)	Matthew 25:10-13
You had His holy Word in your hand	II Timothy 3:16
(You're gonna wish you had listened to me)	Jeremiah 25:4-8
And you lost it...for your self	Matthew 22:11-14
(Tears are gonna fall, not looking for the Son)	Matthew 25:10-13
You would have had it all	Revelation 21:7
Looking for the Son	Titus 2:13, Lk. 21:36
You had His holy Word in your hand	II Timothy 3:16
But you missed it... for your self	Matthew 22:11-14

Lov'n the world....not the open door	I Jn. 2:15, Rev. 4:1
Down the broad way... blind to what life's really for	Matthew 7:13-14
Turn around now...while there still is time	I Jn. 1:9, II Pet. 3:9
Learn your lesson now or you'll reap just what you sow	Galatians 6:7

(You're gonna wish you had listened to me)
You would have had it all
(Tears are gonna fall, not looking for the Son)
You would have had it all
(You're gonna wish you had listened to me)
It all, it all, it all
(Tears are gonna fall, not looking for the Son)

You would have had it all
(You're gonna wish you had listened to me)
Looking for the Son
(Tears are gonna fall, not looking for the Son)
You had His holy Word in your hand
(You're gonna wish you had listened to me)
And you missed it...for your self
(Tears are gonna fall, not looking for the Son)

You would have had it all
(You're gonna wish you had listened to me)
Looking for the Son
(Tears are gonna fall, not looking for the Son)
You had His holy Word in your hand
(You're gonna wish you had listened to me)
But you missed it
You missed it
You missed it
You missed it....for your self

Scripture Summary
Jeremiah 25:4-8
Habakkuk 2:2
Matthew 6:20
Matthew 6:33
Matthew 7:13
Matthew 22:11-14
Matthew 25:10-13
Luke 21:34-36
Luke 24:332
John 3:16-17
I Corinthians 15:52
Galatians 6:7
Philippians 1:3-6
II Timothy 3:16
Titus 2:13
II Peter 3:9
II Peter 3:4
I John 1:9
I John 2:15
Revelation 3:10
Revelation 3:14-22
Revelation 4:1
Revelation 20:4-6
Revelation 21:7
Revelation 22:17

(See www.ProphecyCountdown.com for more information)

www.ingramcontent.com/pod-product-compliance
Lightning Source LLC
Chambersburg PA
CBHW031552040426
42452CB00006B/283